D1596865

ROCK THE RECESSION

ROCK THE RECESSION

HOW SUCCESSFUL LEADERS PREPARE FOR, THRIVE DURING, AND CREATE WEALTH AFTER DOWNTURNS

JONATHAN SLAIN
PAUL BELAIR

ROCK THE RECESSION

How Successful Leaders Prepare for, Thrive
During, and Create Wealth After Downturns

ISBN   978-1-5445-0191-8 *Hardcover*

978-1-5445-0189-5 *Paperback*

978-1-5445-0190-1 *Ebook*

Jonathan's Dedication:

To Paul.

You've changed the course of my life; I am a better husband, father, provider, and person because of you. You even taught me an important lesson when you shellacked me in tennis! Above all, thank you for being my friend without any expectation. This first book is dedicated to you. (Our next book might have to be dedicated to our families or maybe my mother-in-law...)

Paul's Dedication:

To Jonathan.

I know we give each other a hard time a lot and that we almost always joke with each other, but on a serious note, I have thoroughly enjoyed working with you and am lucky to have met you. I'm looking forward to being a small part of you realizing your life-plan dreams!

TABLE OF CONTENTS

TABLE OF QUESTIONS

AUTHORS' NOTE

All stories and interviews in this book are true, to the best of our knowledge. Some names and company names have been changed to protect the identity of contributors who wished to remain anonymous.

INTRODUCTION

ROCK THE RECESSION

JONATHAN: I SURVIVED THE GREAT RECESSION BY BORROWING A QUARTER OF A MILLION DOLLARS FROM MY MOTHER-IN-LAW

Yes, you read that right. I had no plan in place for the recession. I owned a number of franchises of something called Fitness Together. These personal training studios did great at first—we grew very fast, opening several new locations. Our studios achieved new franchise records every year. It felt like we couldn't miss! In 2008, we set a world record for the most personal training sessions ever in the history of the franchise, and later the most locations ever. We just grew and grew and grew...

Until we ran into the Great Recession.

The only reason we survived at all was that I borrowed

over $250,000 from my mother-in-law. Amazingly, I'm still married, and I have paid back what I owed at this point. But it was bad. I wasn't prepared whatsoever: I hadn't been monitoring any of the gauges on the business. Because I had no plan for what to do when the recession hit, I spent the first couple months curled up in the fetal position in the corner of my office.

I couldn't pick my head up—everything collapsed so fast. I wasn't thinking clearly; I was too emotional. Every week, I had to call my mother-in-law for more money. The $250,000 wasn't one big loan. I asked her for $20,000, and then $20,000 more, and then another $20,000. I just kept coming back, week by week, probably a dozen times or more, until she had lent me over a quarter of a million dollars total. I still remember those agonizing phone calls...

Hey Anne (that's my mother-in-law's name)...*the girls are great...yep, really doing well...your daughter is also doing great...*

So I was calling because I was hoping...

I was hoping you could send me another check, so I can make payroll again...

Can you imagine? It was terrible all around. I felt like I

was getting waterboarded by the recession. To complicate matters further, mine was a family business. I had three brothers-in-law, a sister, and a sister-in-law all in the business. Once we reached a certain point during the depths of the recession, we had to make some terrible decisions about who was going to be let go. There was no choice: we just couldn't afford to pay everyone anymore.

Up to this point, our journey had been a happy one. We had started with one location and grown rapidly to five. But then the Great Recession happened—and the wheels came off. The worst part was the emotional toll it took on all of us. Personally, I went through a series of emotional stages: first, feeling like a failure, then questioning why this had happened to me and how I got there. I felt raw and exposed, like all my insecurities had been put on display. My self-worth had been tied up in the business. It all just made me feel like I had failed.

Studies have shown that during a downturn people gravitate toward junk food and tend to overeat. In Alabama, a state that was hit especially hard by the Great Recession, an already alarming obesity problem became even more severe, according to AL.com. I may not live in Alabama, but I can relate. When you're scared and numb, you need *something* to grasp onto. It is a terrible feeling.

> My self-worth had been tied up in my business. I felt
> like a failure.

Luckily, I had a wife and a mother-in-law who believed in
me. But trying to figure out what to do about all my brothers-
in-law was so difficult emotionally, especially knowing we
were all going to have to be together at Thanksgiving. I
was the keystone of the family business, the one who had
brought everyone together in the first place. I felt responsible for what had happened—I needed to figure out a
solution to preserve our increasingly strained relationships.

Ours was a typical family business, and we had made
all the mistakes that family businesses make. Because
we had no plan, there was no path to save ourselves that
didn't involve much pain and emotion. I just remember
us having so many arguments with everyone, including
me, trying to place the blame on someone else.

Looking back now, I see that I made a colossal business
mistake—I clung to our one and only service, our one skill
as a company, which was one-on-one personal fitness
training. To be fair, no matter what I did, I would have
still been swimming against the current. Personal training is probably the worst thing that you can try to sell in
a recession when customers are tightening their belts.
Nobody wants to pay for personal training in a recession
(I can say that now, with 20/20 hindsight).

> *Nobody* wants to pay for personal training in a recession.

But if I hadn't been so busy fighting with my family and battling my own demons, **I could have pivoted and expanded into other services**, like group training. If I had established a plan in advance, I would have been able to lower my prices before it was too late and keep more clients. Or at the very least, I could have limited the borrowing—and wound up owing my mother-in-law a lot less than $250,000!

I also ponder what would have happened if I had been able to read a book like ours back in 2007. I might have been in a much better place. Obviously, that didn't happen. But what *did* happen was that my path crossed with Paul's. After initially coming together through the Young Presidents' Organization (YPO) and Entrepreneurs' Organization (EO) mentorship program, he randomly became my mentor for a year. It was the start of a friendship and partnership that has now lasted close to a decade and is still going strong.

During the past eight years, Paul and I have worked with many of the same clients. We have helped them build value, gain traction, and grow profitably. At some point, I also tried to find resources to help our clients prepare for the next recession. But there was just nothing out there. Nothing on Amazon, nothing on Google for "recession workbook." I said to Paul: "Somebody should really write a book about how to plan for the next recession."

It dawned on us that maybe *we* were "somebody." We started putting together our own recession workbook for clients—the *Rock the Recession Owner's Manual*™—and the feedback was overwhelmingly positive. We realized there was a much larger audience for this message. For reasons that will soon be made clear, Paul was proof that our system worked. His plan—and the process he created—became the foundation of this new Recession Gearbox Model that we began sharing with clients and speaking about publicly in our talks and workshops.

Now, with this book, we are sharing everything we have learned along the way—**everything you need to know about how successful leaders prepare for, thrive during, and create wealth after downturns.**

Our process—the methodology we are putting forth here—can be used at any time, whether there's a recession or not. Furthermore, when we talk about a "recession," we don't just mean a broad economic downturn. **A recession can refer to any big shock to a company's system.**

> When you lose your biggest customer, you're in a recession.

When your best employees leave to open a competing business across the street, you're in a recession. When your key vendor or key supplier cuts you off, you're in a recession. When your partner embezzles from you, you—my friend—are in a recession!

All of which is to say: if you're in business at some point you're *going to* experience a recession in one form or another. It's guaranteed. That is why, no matter how healthy your business is, or you think it is, you should consider creating a recession plan as part of your basic **business hygiene.**

Paul's business, Roth Bros., Inc. (Roth), had a plan. He was looking forward to the recession. He had purchased a company and done very specific things to grow it spectacularly, **using the Great Recession as fuel that led to his American Dream Exit.**

Me? I was only in the personal training business in the first place because my brother-in-law happened to be a fitness guru and I wanted to retire from the investment-banking world. I had no plan for when the recession hit, and our business crashed—almost fatally.

Ours is a tale of two businesses merging onto the freeway right before the Great Recession in 2008. One zoomed ahead and the other—mine—crashed and burned. Learn from my mistakes. **Don't be like me. Be like Paul.** Do recession planning *right*, and you can achieve your own Dream Outcome. But it all starts with you. Who do you want to be when the next downturn comes?

> Do you want to be the car in the fast lane, zooming past everyone, or the car stuck on the side of the road with its engine smoking?

PAUL: MY PLAN FOR THE GREAT RECESSION

I saw a lot of businesses get beaten down during the Great Recession. They didn't have a plan. My team did. In fact, my business—Roth, a national specialty contracting company—grew by double digits right through the Great Recession. We bought the company with $1 million of equity before the downturn. Then, we spent the next sixty-three months growing the business—before finally selling it, after the recession, for more than $70 million, over a seventy times return on investment. This exponential growth was all made possible because we had a plan and we executed it. We performed so well during the recession that we were able to achieve our **American Dream Exit**—selling the business for enough money to be able to do whatever we wanted to do when we wanted to do it.

> We turned $1 million into over $70 million in just a little over five years—all during a tough recession.

How did we do it? One of the key ideas we drew from was Covey's principle: "Begin with the end in mind." When I became one of the owners of the company at age forty-four, I focused not only on my goals but the exit strategy. About a year in, my team started to develop a five-year plan to dramatically increase our performance—and specifically to raise the multiple paid by a buyer if and when we decided to sell.

Having this exit plan from the beginning, not just at the end, was crucial. It led to new insights—a greater understanding of what created value—and drove us to make changes that would someday maximize the sale of our business. Even if we never ended up selling the business, we would still dramatically improve business performance. (Some plans, like exit plans and recession plans, are important to have on hand before you need them.)

> Create value by beginning with the end in mind.

Meanwhile, many of our competitors in the contracting business were **mired in complacency**. Everything was going well for them. Why rock the boat? At least that's how *they* probably thought about the situation.

I see the same complacency whenever times are good. Very few companies **proactively** contemplate how they might survive and thrive during a recession, unless they're actually *in* a downturn (reactionary). Because they're so busy right now, they can't imagine we're headed for another downturn.

And then, of course, there are the companies that haven't been through a recession themselves at all. For them, it's a different situation. It's like the story of the two young fish who are swimming along when they meet an older fish swimming the other way. "Morning, boys," the older fish says. "How's the water?" The two young fish continue swimming until one of them turns to the other and asks, "What's water?"

It's the same with recessions. We could definitely have one coming on, and the younger fish just don't know it because they haven't experienced it yet!

David Rosenberg, Chief Economist and Strategist at Gluskin Sheff (and frequent CNBC commentator), said it best when he tweeted: "'I can't see a recession!—Where's the recession!' I can't tell you how much I hear this every single day. It's like saying 'I can't smell the carbon monoxide.' By the time you 'see the recession,' your head's sliced off."

JONATHAN: OUR BIG IDEA

We want to alert leaders, in all industries, to the importance of having a recession plan *now*. Together, we are driven—Paul and I—by a passion to help others succeed and achieve their own Dream Outcomes. This is what gets us excited. It's what gets me out of bed every morning. **No one should have to borrow money from their mother-in-law!**

Of course, there are ways to become successful other than to leverage the opportunities created by a recession. But if what you're looking for is a genuinely *big* result, a 10X result—a true Dream Outcome—then a recession can do that for you like almost nothing else. (By Dream Outcome, I mean the idea that you can start with little or nothing and build a business that allows you to realize your vision of success—however you define it!)

A recession is like driving on the Autobahn. As crazy as that sounds, it's the best metaphor I can think of. On the Autobahn you are going so fast that, if you don't have a plan, it is easy to crash. And crashing at such a high speed is, of course, devastating. It's the same in a recession. There's no time to think: if you don't act quickly, you lose everything. But if you have a *plan*, you **put yourself in position to pass the competition and zoom toward your Dream Outcome.**

It's all about having a plan—and then *practicing* that plan. Have you ever driven a car with a manual transmission? If so, do you remember what it felt like when you first learned how to shift the gears? Getting comfortable driving stick shift is a lot like recession planning. At first, it feels clumsy and awkward. Your brain works in overdrive trying to remember the sequence: step on the clutch pedal, then shift gears, then let off the clutch, while giving it some gas.

But with practice, you don't even think about it anymore because you create muscle memory. Shifting gears becomes second nature. You're driving down the road, eating a cheeseburger, talking on your cell phone—not even paying attention to the stick shift. You do it all subconsciously. And it's like that with recession planning: it goes from feeling mechanical, artificial, something that makes your brain hurt, to something that is just always there, that you couldn't turn off even if you wanted to. **You start to see opportunities to grow your business in a recession without even thinking about it.**

> Recession planning is like learning to drive stick shift. At first it feels awkward and artificial but with practice it becomes second nature.

THE FOUR GEARS OF RECESSION PLANNING

We all want to be the car that can punch it and slingshot past the competition. But **so many of us are driving around aimlessly with no plan for surviving, let alone thriving during the next downturn.**

The goal of this book is to help you *pounce*—slingshot past the competition—during a recession. And we realize that everyone is coming to the book from a different starting point. Say your company is in a position of financial strength: you have no debt, you have access to a generous line of credit, and you have healthy equity in the business: you are in a great position to pounce during the next recession.

What do we mean by "pounce" in this context? Pouncing is taking advantage of all the businesses who *don't* have your financial strength: by acquiring them, by recruiting the best people away from them, or by being able to buy their assets cheap (when they foreclose on their loans for expensive equipment they bought during flush times).

What if your business is *not* currently in a position of strength? Depending on the economic circumstances, you can still *get* to a position of strength before the next recession if you have the right plan. Many people are in this situation. Maybe they have heavy debt because they grew too fast. Maybe they got carried away and bought a vacation home before they could afford it.

Everyone's situation is different, and you can use this book in different ways depending on the health of your "vehicle" and where you are on the highway. If you are out in front, then you need to be stomping on the accelerator. Now is the time to grow, to maximize opportunity—to really go for it. But if you're stuck behind a pack of other cars, your strategy has to be different. Or, if you're in the race but your engine is starting to smoke, you're going to need to tap the brakes.

To help you understand how to use this book in the way that best suits you—and Choose Your Own Adventure, so to speak—we have put together the following model. This is the way our recession "gearbox" works: the chain represents the economy, and the economy is what drives the gears. The economy, of course, follows a certain cycle, as all economies do: it is always in a state of expansion, recovery, contraction, or recession.

There are four gears in the gearbox. They are: 1st. Assess, 2nd. Tune, 3rd. Race, and 4th. Accelerate. Always start in 1st Gear and then, depending on the state of the economy, you're going to want to shift to 2nd, 3rd, or 4th Gear.

For example, if the economy is in expansion or recovery, you'll engage 1st Gear and then 2nd Gear. You're going to want to start by assessing your situation and then tuning up your engine. From there, you'll shift to 3rd Gear and 4th Gear. If the economy is in recovery or contraction, though, you'll want to start in 1st Gear and then go straight to 3rd Gear and then move on to 4th Gear. If the economy is in contraction or recession, you'll want to start in 1st Gear and then shift directly to 4th Gear. In a contraction, you'll need to use your judgment to select between 3rd and 4th Gear based on how quickly the economy is shrinking.

You're *always* going to start in 1st Gear. In fact, 1st Gear is external to the economy. No matter where you are in the economic cycle, it is vital that you start by assessing your situation. You can't even get on the highway if you don't understand where you are, where you want to go, and how far ahead or behind you are—and you do this by benchmarking your recession readiness against others in your industry. This assessment is how you identify opportunities for improvement.

And in 1st Gear, you need to assess not only your situation but also your self-awareness. Do you understand the economy and what it means for your business? Do you know what to look for? Do you know what it means when the ten-year and two-year US treasury bond yields invert?

> The four gears of the Recession Gearbox Model are: Assess, Tune, Race, and Accelerate.

Now you know the four gears, but there is another important part of the model: the **Emergency Brake**. If you're in 3rd Gear or 4th Gear and it's just not working, you're not able to continue racing or accelerating, you may have to pull the Emergency Brake to save the business. But again, you only yank this lever in specific circumstances: namely, when your business is in a recession and racing or accelerating isn't working.

The most important thing to recognize now is this: **one of the cardinal rules of the road is to know your destination and how you're going to get there before you begin.** Which means that regardless of whether your balance sheet is strong or not so strong—and whether we're in a recession or recovery—you must have a written plan in place. And you must understand *where you are now.*

How do you determine that? By doing our Recession Readiness Assessment™. As far as we know, it's the only assessment of its kind in the world! And, so far, we've collected tons of responses from a wide swath of business leaders. This data allows us to understand and share with you, the reader, how prepared you are for a recession versus everyone else that has taken the assessment.

HOMEWORK: YOUR ASSESSMENT

The following is a twenty-question exercise designed to assess where you are in your recession readiness. (Note that you and your team can also take this assessment for free at www.recession.com/ready if you prefer.) The higher the score, the better positioned you are to pounce!

Recession Readiness Assessment

Complete online at www.Recession.com/ready

Name _____ Date _____

Company_____ Position _____

Our goal is to ensure you are in the best position to capture the opportunities a recession brings. One of the first steps in our journey together is for you to benchmark your company's "recession readiness."

Readiness is defined as the state of being fully prepared. Our Recession Readiness Assessment will give you a quantified answer for just how prepared you are for the next downturn. This assessment is a systematic analysis of your company's ability to perform, removing guesswork and emotion, which will allow you to identify strengths and potential challenges for your company in the next downturn.

Once you have this information, you will be ready to hit the road armed with the knowledge of where you want to go and guidance from us on how to get there.

. . . .

INSTRUCTIONS:

Please take approximately 10 minutes of uninterrupted time to complete the assessment. Answer the 20 items using the following scale:

GREEN: YES/ALWAYS

YELLOW: MAYBE/SOMETIMES

RED: NO/NEVER

WHITE: Wave this flag if you don't understand the question or if you honestly have no idea how to answer. We encourage you to use this option if it applies, as waving the white flag will result in the best possible recommendations for you and your company.

Once complete, you will receive an email with your results and score.

. . . .

Recession Readiness Assessment

Complete online at www.Recession.com/ready

 1st GEAR ASSESS

	YES/ ALWAYS	MAYBE/ SOME	NO/ NEVER	I DON'T KNOW

1. Does your company have a written action plan for the next recession or major shock to your company's system (i.e., losing your biggest customer)?

2. Does your company's leadership team understand and track basic economic indicators (for example, the yield curve and the unemployment rate)?

3. Are your company's vision, mission, and values documented in writing and exemplified daily through behaviors at all levels of the company?

4. Does your company have a written, long-term, focused strategic plan and do you spend at least one day each quarter updating it?

 2nd GEAR TUNE

5. Does your company's leadership team understand the financial health of its major customers and vendors?

6. Is your company's EBITDA (Earnings Before Interest, Taxes, Depreciation, and Amortization) margin "best in class" for your industry?

7. Does your company have five to ten percent of its next twelve months of estimated revenue as equity on your balance sheet?

8. Does your company's leadership team regularly meet with its bank representatives to discuss the company's line of credit to ensure the limit is right for current and future business needs?

9. Does your company's leadership team know all restrictions in place on any company debt and do they review these "covenants" monthly to ensure compliance?

10. Do your company's owners regularly review any personal guarantees on company debt and are they actively working to reduce them to zero?

Recession Readiness Assessment
Complete online at www.Recession.com/ready

	YES/ ALWAYS	MAYBE/ SOME	NO/ NEVER	I DON'T KNOW

11. Does your company have cash or debt available to fund growth?

12. Does your company have a board of advisors that meets at least quarterly with the leadership team to help set plans for growth, ask challenging questions, and hold the team accountable for its action plans?

3 | 3rd GEAR | RACE

13. Do you have an excellent company culture, hire only awesome people, and immediately exit people who are not awesome or who don't fit your culture?

14. Does your company have a continuous improvement process in place and do you regularly measure progress against established goals?

15. Does your company's leadership team have an accurate method of tracking its backlog, its current work in progress, and its pipeline of potential new work?

16. Does your company have a method to track the productivity of each employee?

17. Does your company's leadership team compare actual financial results achieved against intended results at the completion of each project or quarter (whichever is most appropriate for your business)?

4 | 4th GEAR | ACCELERATE

18. Is your company's customer base diversified?

19. Is your company's revenue diversified? Do you serve some market sectors that are counter-cyclical or unaffected by recessions?

EMERGENCY BRAKE

20. Does your company's leadership team have a way to measure for early warning signs that your business is headed in the wrong direction?

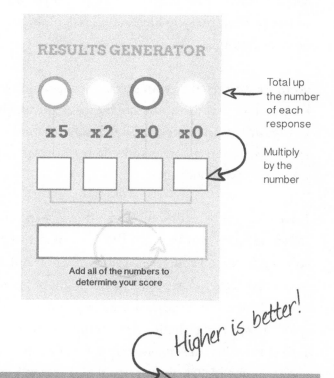

RESULTS GENERATOR

Total up the number of each response

x5 x2 x0 x0

Multiply by the number

Add all of the numbers to determine your score

Higher is better!

85 - 100 = LOOKING FORWARD to the next Recession!

60 - 84 = Need to START PREPARING for the next Recession!

0 - 59 = High risk of FAILURE in the next Recession!

How did you score? If your tally was 85 or higher, congrats, you should be *looking forward* to the next recession! If it was between 60 and 84, it's definitely time for you to *start preparing* for the recession. And if you scored 59 or lower, beware—you have a real risk of *failure* in the next recession.

Were you surprised by your score? Most people are—and that is exactly why the assessment is so critical. **Human beings are just not very reliable judges.** Actually, we're really *bad* when it comes to knowing how we're doing relative to everybody else.

Have you ever been driving on the freeway and changed lanes because you thought the lane next to you was moving faster? Of course—we all have, right? But did you know researchers have studied this habit of lane changing and found that the vast majority of drivers are not good at predicting whether or not other lanes are moving faster? In reality, the lanes are usually all moving at about the same speed. The perception that one lane is moving faster is nothing more than an illusion.

Just like with driving, we are very bad judges when it comes to assessing ourselves and our businesses. So if you expected to score high on the assessment and didn't, that's completely normal. Happily, no matter where you fall in the range of results, you can still become recession ready—but you *have* to have a written plan. If you don't, then you're not even in the race. You're standing on the berm of the highway watching others go by. That may be just fine for you. Your vision of success may not be to 10X your business. Not everyone has it in them to sling-shot past their competition. But if your Dream Outcome includes high net profit from your business, you need to focus on getting your recession readiness responses to be all green. You can use this book and the companion *Rock the Recession* workbook to achieve your goal.

Stakes are high: having a plan can mean the difference between bankruptcy and a Dream Outcome. Sure, you may still survive without one. You may not go bankrupt, but I wouldn't count on it. Not everyone is lucky enough to have a generous mother-in-law to bail them out. In fact, I even wrote something to that effect in one of my letters to her: "Most businesses don't have the aid of a benefactor to help them grow when times are good and to lend a hand when times are tough." Looking back, what I really needed wasn't a benefactor—what I needed was a plan.

One thing is for sure: if you're not ready for the trip—if you're just letting the business happen *to* you—you're unlikely to achieve your own **Dream Outcome**.

What does "Dream Outcome" mean to you? Let your imagination roam free here. What if the gears you are learning about in this book could help you afford the car or house of your dreams? Better yet, what if they could help you achieve financial independence many years earlier than you thought possible? Or what if these gears could _____ (you fill in the blank)?

Have we gotten your attention yet? Assuming you *want* to be on the highway to your Dream Outcome, now is your time. **We are calling on you to join us for the trip of a lifetime.** If you're like a lot of the people we talk to, you were hit hard in the last recession. Maybe it took you a long time to recover, and now you don't know how to prevent it from happening again. We get it; that's why we wrote this book.

Often we ask audiences a series of questions: do you believe the next recession will increase, decrease, or have no effect on your profit (decrease); do you have a written plan at your company for the next recession (no); finally, we ask if they're *looking forward* to the next recession (hell no). We get a lot of raised eyebrows with that one. **Who on earth would look forward to a recession?**

Us—that's who! And so will you, by the end of this book.

Do you believe the next recession will increase, decrease or have no effect on your profit?

INCREASE 5%

DECREASE - 66%

NO EFFECT - 29%

Source Recession.com

Do you have a written plan at your company for the next recession?

YES - 1%

NO - 99%

Source Recession.com

When everyone else is making drastic cuts, worried about surviving, hoping to ride out the recession by retreating into their shell like a turtle—turtling up—you'll be ready to pounce!

The first step is to take what you've learned from your Recession Readiness Assessment and use it to start mapping out the basic contours of your recession plan.

Buckle up!

CHAPTER ONE

1ST GEAR—ASSESS

Instructions for using **The Recession Gearbox:**

⚙ 1st Gear (Assess) Always start with 1st Gear

⚙ Then engage 2nd Gear (Tune), 3rd Gear (Race), and/or 4th Gear (Accelerate) depending on "The Economy"

- If the Economy is in the Expansion or Recovery stages of the cycle, engage 2nd Gear, then 3rd Gear, then 4th Gear
- If the Economy is in Recovery or Contraction, engage 3rd Gear, then 4th Gear
- If the Economy is in Contraction or Recession, engage 4th Gear immediately if possible

🔒 Use the Emergency Brake at any point if needed

And, above all else, use your judgment to determine which Gear to use given the circumstances within your company and outside in The Economy

PAUL: HOW I COMMITTED TO WIN

In 1999, when I took over the reins as president of Roth—a national specialty contractor founded in 1923—it became clear to me that our vision needed to be recalibrated. I had inherited a company that was overly reliant on heating, ventilation, and air conditioning (HVAC) construction and had many C-players in that segment of the business.

Because I came to Roth from an accounting (CPA) and business background (MBA), I was able to **assess** the situation in an analytical, unemotional way. I knew that construction—which made up 80 percent of our business at that point—was normally a very low-margin, high-risk business. I also saw the value in our *service* offerings: HVAC services, roofing services, and energy management. The service side of our business was an annuity business, which means that the service is normally renewed each year.

Finally, I looked at what we were doing with our energy management and energy monitoring products, and how we could rebrand those divisions with our other service products around green energy and conservation. All in all, after surveying our entire business landscape, my team and I came to the conclusion that a major restructuring was in order.

If I had been a "status quo guy"—the kind of person who doesn't like to rock the boat and is fine just chugging along with a low-margin business—I might not have set my sights on reshaping the company to the degree that I did. But I was used to change and making hard decisions, having been a leader in my previous role as CFO for a private equity portfolio company.

> Shaking things up (restructuring) is just something you have to do to a business every five to ten years.

But that didn't mean the restructuring came easily. I had to select a new management team from the talent within the company, a new leadership team, and set in motion a process for us to thrive. I had to let go of a number of long-term employees. Layoffs were something that never happened at Roth, but I knew what had to be done. I had to shut down offices in various cities (sites where they were focused on our construction division). I did it all at once. I knew **I had to rip off the Band-Aid so we could all focus on the future**.

Through this whole period, I took the layoffs very personally: I knew I was impacting people's families and livelihoods. There were days that just flat-out sucked. But through it all, I trusted I was doing the right thing. I had to set the company on a growth path and eliminate any culture of mediocrity that might have been seeping in—to instill in its place a culture of growth and customer-service excellence.

Looking back now, I can safely say that the painful experience was worth it. Again, if I were a status quo guy, I would probably still be working in that business today instead of playing Pickleball in Southwest Florida. And I certainly wouldn't have had my successful exit. No one wants to buy an average business.

In order to achieve your Dream Outcome, you need to **commit to win.** And to win, you need to *prepare.*

After His Dream Exit from Roth Bros., Paul Is Now Committed to Win at Pickleball/Paul Belair

COMMITTING TO *PREPARATION*

Committing to preparation means making a formal plan. In this chapter, we show you exactly how to create a **written action plan** to prepare your company for recession.

Why do you need a recession plan? After all, your business may be doing great right now, with high revenue, record profit, and a strong backlog, and you can't even imagine a downturn. If that's the case, congratulations on your success so far. We hate to rain on your parade; however, it's important you understand a **recession is inevitable**. It's simple economics. Recessions happen cyclically; every peak is followed by a valley. The only questions are: *when are we at the peak,* and *how long will the good times last?*

It's like the seasons of the year. It's not up for debate that winter is coming. It's just a question of how bad it's going to be and for how long. (Interesting factoid: as a society we talk less about climate change during a recession, probably because everybody's focused on turning the economy around and because there's little money for new investment in green technology. According to Boston College's Xiaorui Huang, "recessions lower the prominence of climate change in political and public discourse.")

> The next recession isn't a matter of "if." It's always a matter of "when."

When recessions happen, the economy makes what we call a "**Pit Stop**." Trade and industrial activity decline, income falls, the gross domestic product (GDP) stays low for a period of time (technically, a recession is when GDP falls for two successive quarters).

You may think the economy still has enough gas for you to run a few more laps around the track before the Pit Stop—and maybe you're right. But even if you disagree that a broad economic downturn is coming, you and your company could still hit a recession at any time. Remember, you can go into recession after something as commonplace as losing a major customer. Any Black-Swan event in your business can throw you into a recession. (A Black Swan, according to author Nassim Taleb in his book *Black Swan*, is a highly improbable event that: 1. is unpredictable, 2. carries massive impact, and 3. after it's over, we invent an explanation for why it was more probable than it really was.) It's not just about waiting for the entire economy to falter, because all companies go through boom times and through recessionary times. So **if you think you don't need a recession plan because you're already "recession proof," think again.**

Take our friend Sebastian, for example. He owns a large commercial landscaping company that has been around for thirty years; and, for nearly twenty of those years his company has used the H-2B guest worker visa program to hire workers from Mexico. Due to policy/regulatory changes, however, his application in 2018 was denied. What happened? He experienced a recession. He didn't have a written plan for what he would do if his access to the foreign-worker program was discontinued. When it was, he was left scrambling.

What could Sebastian have done differently? In his industry, as it turns out, these changes didn't create massive winners and losers. Basically everybody in the landscaping business was affected at the same time. But imagine what would have been possible if Sebastian had already established a recession plan before the H-2B program was shut down. Instead of playing defense and running around in circles (scrambling to find almost eighty new people to hire in only two months!), he could have switched into execution mode. He could have been ready to pounce—to nab great workers from his competitors, gain new accounts, and expand his business. He could have turned an industry-wide crisis into an opportunity, a chance to buy out other landscapers and bring their customers into his fold.

Because he didn't think of these things in advance—and formalize them in a written plan—he was **too late to pounce on those opportunities.**

> If you don't have a recession plan, you aren't giving yourself a chance to pounce.

JONATHAN: SOME LEADERS HAVE A PLAN

Another business owner I got to know, John, owner of a giant billboard company, actually did have a recession plan but just hadn't documented it. I met John on a flight from Cleveland to Houston. I was working on recession stuff and he looked over and asked me about it.

John is the Billboard King of Texas. He jokingly calls himself a "visual polluter," and has been in the business for forty years, with over five hundred billboards. Hearing about my line of work, he began talking about how he could predict when the next recession was going to come. He described his company as being in the "mood business." He and his team knew what was going on with the economy based on how many billboard renewals they got (when the economy slows down, billboard renewals slow down).

Over forty years, John has seen many ups and downs in business. He learned his lessons the hard way through three recessions (according to John, the one in the early eighties was the worst). He is not invested in the stock market because he doesn't trust it. He trusts in his own personal assets, his billboards and his real estate, and he has put away enough cash that his retirement is secure.

What I like about John is that even though he doesn't have a formal, written plan in the exact way we suggest, he does have a lot of experience with recessions and is making wise decisions based on that experience. In his own way, he actually does have a plan. "If you've never experienced a downturn," says John, "and you're in a growth economy, then you assume it's just going to keep going. People get strung out and they don't know when to cut off the spigot." John has a plan for when to shut off the spigot!

HOW COMMON IS IT TO HAVE A RECESSION PLAN?

We'll put it this way: over the past few years, as we've been crisscrossing the country, talking to CEOs, business leaders, and executives, we always make a point of asking who in the audience has a written recession plan—and very few people raise their hands!

We also ask whether they think the next recession will increase, decrease, or keep profits the same for their businesses. Almost two-thirds—66 percent—say that a recession will decrease their profits. Let that sink in. These leaders believe the recession is going to be bad for them—and yet none of them have a plan to do anything about it!

Unfortunately, they're probably right about the next recession decreasing their profits. According to a 2010 *Harvard Business Review* article, only about 9 percent of the companies surveyed "flourished" after a slowdown. Would that number be higher today? Probably not. In the same article, the authors pointed to how little research had been done on "strategies that can help companies survive a recession, get ahead during a slow-growth recovery, and be ready to win when good times return."

Is there more research available today? Not really. But there is *one* exception to this dearth of material: our research. We have done original research and surveyed tons of companies about their plans for the next recession. This book and its companion workbook, in fact, are drawn from the results of that work.

To put it plainly: the next recession is indeed coming, and more than likely, it will only be about 9 percent of companies, once again, who flourish after the downturn—we want you, with our help, to be part of that 9 percent. Again, hardly any of the people we surveyed have a written plan to survive a recession, much less capitalize on it! That information alone puts you at a distinct advantage. **Now, what are you going to do about it?**

WHAT IS A RECESSION PLAN?

A recession plan is a written document with planned action items. What makes it so vital is that it's created in the cool, rational light of day, *before it's needed*—not in the heat of the night, when passion and emotion are highest.

Why does this matter? Think about landscaper Sebastian again. When he got the bad news, it was almost too much to deal with—understandably so. There were *no* good answers. He was losing the highly experienced H-2B workers he had known for years. In total, he was losing over one thousand years of experience overnight! He became overwhelmed. What was he going to do? How was he going to get through the season?

As time went on, it got even worse. His replacement hires wouldn't show up to work. He had over five hundred call-offs and no-shows. He ended up having to work in the field himself for the first time in twenty years—the only upside was that he lost thirty pounds from all the stress and physical labor.

Sebastian ended up surviving his recession and is now rebuilding his company from the ground up to be nimble and built for the long term. The reason Sebastian persevered is because of his will to succeed and the people, processes, and culture he developed.

When you're in such a stressful situation, naturally it's hard to make good decisions. You're in a defensive posture, crouched in the fetal position. "It's hard to read the label when you're inside the jar," as author Dave Rendell puts it. But when you have a recession plan in place, you are on offense. You know what you have to do and you're ready to do it. This preparation gives you confidence and peace of mind.

"That's why contingency planning is so important," says CJ Rhoads, author of *The Entrepreneur's Guide to Running a Business*. "Strong leaders already have, in their back pocket, a Plan B, and a Plan C, and a D, E, F, and G. When a crisis hits, there is no time to lose. We can't wait for the problem to develop the relationships necessary to solve it. Those relationships must already exist."

According to x10 Consulting's Herm J. Schneider, "Most business leaders should be aware that some of their direct competitors are actually, paradoxically, looking forward to the next recession. Companies with this approach have already learned that by preparing ahead, they can seize the market, while others in the same business struggle during the downturn due to their lack of planning. These high performing organizations have already established the core competencies necessary to identify and anticipate directional shifts in the business cycle."

RECESSION READINESS ASSESSMENT (RRA) QUESTION #1

Does your company have a written action plan for the next recession or major shock to your company's system (e.g., losing your biggest customer)?

Here and throughout the Recession Readiness Assessment (RRA) you're going to be scoring yourself green, yellow, or red. For example, if you're green on question #1, it means you're in great shape. Keep doing what you're doing! But try to take it to the next level by looking at how we describe the green response and using it as inspiration. We'll show you what we mean...

On RRA question #1, a great example of a green response can be seen with Paul's company, Roth. As we know, he had a written action plan for the next recession and he executed it. He took talent that was in his construction division and reassigned those A-players to his recurring revenue services in anticipation of changing wants and needs in a recession. Paul and his team knew that in a recession, HVAC service, energy management, and maintenance would be much more in demand than HVAC construction. In a downturn, customers want to maintain existing equipment (service), not install expensive new equipment (construction).

During the recession, they executed their plan and rebranded the company—"*Roth: Powered by Green*"—to emphasize sustainability and demand-side energy management their services could provide to customers. They started to price proposals in terms of return on investment (ROI) and focused on trying to understand the time frame their customers wanted for their ROI to be realized through energy and maintenance savings. Because of the shift Roth made, the company started getting paid for its intellectual capital, which increased its margins.

Roth was fortunate the recession hit after the company had made this conversion (from focusing on construction to focusing on service). Many of their clients were scaling back any new building, but they *were* maintaining existing spaces—and looking to cut costs. Using its recession plan, Roth flipped its relationships: **the company went from being "just a contractor" to being a "partner" with its clients—working with them to reduce their energy and maintenance expenditures and bringing them value-added ideas.**

Does Paul's story resonate with you? If you have a written action plan you feel confident you can leverage in the way Roth did, score yourself GREEN on RRA question #1.

If you're like most companies, however, you're not quite there yet. You have some kind of strategic plan, but it's not a dedicated, written action plan for the next recession. You haven't benchmarked yourself against your competition. You don't yet fully understand the levers that will increase the value of your company in a recession—and you probably aren't ready to reallocate talent to those areas in support of a broader strategic plan to increase the value of your business. If this sounds like you, score yourself YELLOW on this question.

What should you do, then, to get to where you want to be? If you're yellow on your written action plan, you need to start benchmarking yourself against your competitors, identifying the gaps where those companies are doing better than you. Look at what levers maximize the value of your business and where you are with respect to those levers. Only by identifying these gaps can you start implementing strategies to close them.

Finally, if you have no written plan at all for the next recession—which was basically the situation Jonathan was in with Fitness Together—you're in the RED zone. Call 911! The real danger here is that you lack awareness. Too many companies don't achieve awareness until they're actually in a recession (whether it's an economic recession or just their company facing a sudden internal downturn), at which point it's too late.

You wouldn't want to change a tire when you're on the highway going seventy miles per hour. That's exactly what it's going to feel like if you try to create your recession plan during a recession. Remember: you need to have a plan that is created in the cool, rational light of day, not the emotional heat of the night. And you want to discuss and practice the plan now, so you can move swiftly to execution when it's needed, not spend time convincing your team—and yourself—that it's time to act.

If you scored yourself *red* on this question, it's up to you to take action, quick! Get a copy of the *Rock the Recession Owner's Manual* and start completing the workbook exercises with your leadership team.

> Advance preparation and documentation are critical for thriving during any downturn.

DON'T BURN DOWN THE HOUSE!

During a recession, you may find yourself wanting to burn down your business. It's an understandable impulse! We've all heard stories about how people try to get insurance money this way. Research shows people actually don't commit this crime any more frequently during a recession than when the economy is strong. University of Texas's Zachary A. Powell conducted a twelve-year study to see if these arson-for-profit incidents went up during periods of economic decline and found no correlation. Nonetheless, if you *are* considering burning down your business, please holster your matches—there is a better way!

As we'll see later on, when we talk about creating your recession plan's "Emergency Brake," part of the process involves writing down "tiers" (tiered cuts) to be activated when certain predetermined metrics are reached. If you set your tiers right, you will stay calm and not be tempted to make any rash (not to mention dangerous and illegal) moves like committing insurance fraud! A recession plan works best if you **build your tiers *ahead of time*.**

It's one way to save you from yourself!

What do we mean by that? As humans, our brains are hard-wired to react to a crisis by slamming on the brakes. Strangely enough, we see something similar in human sexuality. According to Emily Nagoski, author of *Come as You Are*, the brain's excitement system (which is responsible for turning us on) is like the gas pedal on a car, and its inhibition system (which turns us off) is like the brakes. Counterintuitively, it's the turn*offs* that carry the most power and have the biggest impact on us. (In Kate Julian's cover story in *The Atlantic*, appropriately titled "The Sex Recession," she draws on this research to examine the phenomenon of young people withdrawing from intimacy.)

It's not just sex! We see the same patterns in ourselves with other kinds of feelings as well: negative emotions are generally stronger and more visceral than positive ones.

What do these biases have to do with recessions? They can steer us off-track if we're not mindful. Recessions are an emotional warzone. The beauty of having a tiered plan, in case of emergency, is that it eliminates the stressful, sometimes heart-wrenching decisions that leaders usually have to make during these times. Because everything has been laid out in advance, there's no uncertainty about what needs to be done. All that remains is to execute if and when the time ever comes (and recessions always come around).

We see a great example of advance planning by another friend of ours, Don Greenland, who was COO of a large, highly successful general contracting firm. More than a decade ago, they created their own version of a recession plan, called the Nabholz Economic Downturn Strategy. While the document differs in some ways from what we are recommending here, the similarities are striking. He and his company made a plan based on different tiers, with specific cuts and reductions associated with each one—and tailored to all the different business units and office locations within the sprawling organization.

The plan also included best practices, meant to be done *at all times*, as well as growth opportunities for the company to consider in the event of a recession, such as new technologies and equipment and new sectors to expand into.

Don's company saw the Great Recession coming and started making changes in advance—keeping their organizational chart flat and maintaining lean overhead, which allowed them to remain competitive in order to get more work into their backlog. This savvy planning allowed the company to keep its best people during the recession and also attract new talent because they had projects to keep people working and their competitors didn't. They ended up hiring many A-players this way. Recessions are like that. But the real point of the story is that they had a plan and they worked it.

Whereas landscaper Sebastian was caught off guard by his (non-economic) recession, Don's company thought things through in advance, put together a plan, and implemented it. In so doing, they were able to capitalize on the opportunities to hire great people. Since then, they have used their Nabholz Economic Downturn Strategy to great advantage and, of course, they keep it updated so it always represents the company's present-day reality.

> Without a plan, recessions are scary. With a plan, recessions offer massive opportunities.

HOW DO YOU KNOW WHEN A RECESSION IS COMING?

No one knows for sure when the next recession is going to hit, and this book is not meant to be a deep dive into forecasting. However, in order to make the best use of your recession plan, it's important to know which indicators to monitor. Assessing your company's recession readiness requires you to first assess your own economic awareness.

There are *many* different indicators you can look at to gauge where the economy is going, from unemployment to consumer confidence to household debt and more. There was even an article in the *Journal of Economic Psychology* that made a strong case for being able to predict recessions based on "pessimistic ruminations in popular songs."

The writer of this improbable piece, Harold M. Zullow, argues that repetition of pessimistic words and phrases in popular songs puts the country in a bad mood—and when the national mood swings negative, it means we're about nine months out from a recession. Americans hear these songs and start to tighten up. For example, the recession of 1969–1970 came right off the heels of Credence Clearwater Revival's hit "Bad Moon Rising," the lyrics of which are chock-full of pessimistic rumination: "I see a bad moon a-rising/I see trouble on the way/I see earthquakes and lightning/I see bad times today."

Of course, there is a self-fulfilling prophecy element to all of this and not only in regard to sad songs. When consumers hear bad news about the economy and start to worry about their personal finances, they stop spending. Stores, in turn, stop stocking as much inventory. Manufacturers are forced to slow down production. All of which can lead to recession.

Again, there are no easy answers when it comes to predicting the next recession or knowing whether to be optimistic or pessimistic in the face of different kinds of evidence. What's important is that you understand *it's going to happen*. Again, it's a matter of when, not if. To hope that it's coming later rather than sooner is not good enough. As author and financial expert John Mauldin likes to say: "hope is not a strategy."

According to Mauldin, "Whenever it happens, the next downturn will hit millions who still haven't recovered from the last recession, millions more who did recover but forgot how bad it was, and millions more who reached adulthood before the boom."

So how are *you* going to know when it's going to happen? According to a 2006 article by John A. Pearce II and Steven C. Michael, even professional economists have a hard time identifying and predicting recessions. They point out that a full six months after the commencement of the US recession that began in 2001, a full 90 percent of economists did not believe the United States was in one!

So yes, even the experts get it wrong. Nonetheless, we are confident that, for the purpose of this book, there is one very important indicator of an upcoming recession you can look to reliably—and know with relative certainty a downturn is imminent. We are talking here about the **yield curve**.

If you're only going to be looking at one metric to predict a recession, this is the one. What *is* a yield curve? Think of it like this: if you are holding a ten-year loan, clearly you should get paid a higher interest rate than if it were a two-year loan, right? Even if you knew nothing about economics, you would agree with that. It's no different than if your friend said, "Hey, spot me $500, and I'll pay you back in a year." You would want to get your money back with interest versus if they were going to pay you back next week!

When that *doesn't* happen, when you get paid more interest for short-term loans than long-term loans, it's a big deal. You see it on the news. We call it an inversion, an inverted yield curve. It indicates economic uncertainty and often an expected slowdown in the economy.

How long after an inversion until a full-blown recession? Historically, it happens between ten and twenty-two months later. If you watch and pay attention for that inverted yield curve on the news, you'll have some indication we're getting closer to a recession—and can plan accordingly.

Does your company's leadership team understand and track basic economic indicators (for example, the yield curve and the unemployment rate)?

Here, once again, a great example of a company that scores GREEN is Paul's company, Roth. When he became president, Paul was an unusual addition to the team, having both a CPA and an MBA at a construction company. This is not the typical background for a leader of a national specialty contractor. But it served the company well. Paul's strength is macroeconomics, finance, and strategy. He was the right person at the right time to proactively be reading the economic tea leaves.

And that's what you'll need as well. If you scored yourself green here, it means you understand how the economy affects your business. Which is great—keep it up! A word of caution though: what we've found is many companies *think* they have this covered, when in reality they don't have the necessary internal resources (aka someone like Paul). Because of this, they don't know what they don't know, which is the most dangerous position of all.

If you're only watching a few indicators without really investing time thinking about how they impact your business, score yourself YELLOW. You need to go find and use external advisors to fill this gap. Who in your network has their finger on the pulse of the economy, knows how it may impact your company, and can help you avoid being blindsided? Go find that person, reach out to them, and glean everything you can from their experience and knowledge.

What you *don't* want to do, once again, is be like Jonathan. At Fitness Together, Jonathan was a definite red on this question. He wasn't staying up to speed with economic indicators. Nobody on the management team was going about the necessary research in any kind of intentional way. At best, they were occasionally paying attention to what was going on with unemployment. But they lacked *action*.

If you're in a similar situation, if you're RED on this question, you're behind the curve. You're reactive instead of proactive, and will likely have to cut overhead, reduce headcount, and hunker down when the next recession hits. Once indicators suggest we're in a downturn, it's way too late to capitalize on the myriad of opportunities. Follow the recommendations for yellow now or prepare to make painful cuts in the next recession. Check out www.recession.com for more resources.

Are you with us so far? Good.

Now, how do you go about actually creating your plan?

YOUR RECESSION PLAN

In order to create a recession plan, first you need to get the lay of the land within your organization. You have already filled out your Recession Readiness Assessment. Now, to complete this process of *benchmarking* your company's recession readiness versus your competitors, you need to gather the necessary facts and figures to assess what you'll need in your plan.

First, collect your current financial statements, including your income statement (down to expense line items), balance sheet, cash flow statement, equipment/asset inventory, backlog, and work in progress (WIP)[1]. Second, look at your history from prior years: your old income statements, your past backlog, and WIP reports. What are the trends you see?

Do you know how much your company is currently worth? Consult your financial advisors for a quick estimate. You'd be surprised by how many owners don't know this number or range, which is why they never take the steps necessary to dramatically increase their company's value. It's all about understanding where you are now and what will drive up the value of your company.

---

1   WIP applies usually to contractors or manufacturers.

Next, gather your list of current employees and make sure the list includes name, department, salary/total compensation, and tenure. Gather all of your strategic planning documents concerning mission, vision, values, and goals. Finally, put together a list of your top twenty customers (company, revenue, gross margin, and net profit) and top twenty vendors (company and total annual spend with each).

Now that you have all this information, what do you with it? As we'll see in the following chapters, there's no one-size-fits-all solution. But, according to the 2010 *Harvard Business Review* article mentioned earlier in this chapter, **the companies that have the best performance in sales and EBITDA (Earnings Before Interest, Taxes, Depreciation, and Amortization) after a recession are the ones that focus simultaneously on three things: increasing operational efficiency, developing new markets, and enlarging their asset base.** That combination has proven to be ideal according to HBR—and in our own research as well.

> Clearly, it's time to toss out the conventional wisdom that the best move in a recession is to simply fire people and cut overhead.

‚‚‚‚‚‚‚‚‚‚‚‚‚

Are your company's vision, mission, and values documented in writing and exemplified daily through behaviors at all levels of the company?

Even though Fitness Together had no recession plan, amazingly enough they did have a vision, mission, and values. They used the book *Traction* by Gino Wickman as their guiding methodology and held meetings each quarter to talk about their Core Values, Core Focus™, their 10-Year Target™, and strategies to get there. This is what GREEN on question #3 looks like.

Paul also used a book, *Blue Ocean Strategy*, as a framework for strategic planning and drew from it to conduct brainstorming sessions with the company's leadership team as well as direct reports to the leadership team. The big idea was to identify where their business was suffering by competing on price for commodity work (the bloody red ocean). They examined their assets and talent, and then engaged the leadership team to create uncontested market space (a blue ocean) using their intellectual property to make their competition irrelevant.

This strategic planning proved invaluable. Roth changed course using energy and maintenance savings and return on investment as their key differentiators. They leveraged their in-house talent, along with their intellectual capital to help their customers reduce their energy usage; they became *partners* with their customers.

Even if you scored yourself green here, when it comes to strategic planning we encourage you to stay open to learning more. Consider hiring a consultant to guide one of your strategic planning meetings. Great consultants conduct a high volume of strategic planning sessions each year and can bring your team fresh ideas like Blue Ocean Planning to help your team move further faster! And remember that you get what you pay for, so budget accordingly. If you hire a consultant or coach, you are entrusting them with your most important asset, your business. Vet and select them accordingly.

You need to have a tight, intentional focus. If you don't, score yourself YELLOW. There are many leaders out there who fall into this category. They are aware of the importance of having a vision, mission, and values, but don't think it applies to them. Either that, or they're overly optimistic and just believe everything is going to work out. Or they think they are too busy to spend time on planning. A costly (potentially fatal) mistake.

That's not good enough. If you gave yourself a yellow on this question, you're going to have to pull together an external and internal advisor team and start working on your benchmarking. This is also a great time to start using the Entrepreneurial Operating System® (EOS® aka "Traction") in your business and become really intentional about what you want to be and where you want to drive your company in the next three to five years. EOS® is one of many business operating systems that is proven to help stabilize and grow your business.

Keep it simple and powerful. Your vision, mission, and values should only be one page long. It's not about writing a manifesto that just sits on your server somewhere and no one ever reads. The point is to be clear and concise. Your plan is poetry; every word matters. It's your opportunity to tell your unique story to the world—both internal and external audiences.

Finally, if you currently have no vision in writing, you are RED on this question. Don't think you're just going to get lucky without putting in the work. As Thomas Jefferson said, "I'm a great believer in luck, and I find the harder I work the more I have of it." A great economy may lift all boats, but in a bad economy, according to Warren Buffett, the tide goes out and you see who's been swimming naked.

> If you've been working without a strategic plan, you are swimming naked.

You now have the self-awareness to make a change. Go ahead and start implementing the recommendations for yellow, but realize it's going to be a long journey (at least two years). Check out www.recession.com for more resources.

JONATHAN: WHY IT'S SO IMPORTANT TO HAVE THE RIGHT PEOPLE IN THE ROOM

I had been hired by a large national electrical subcontractor to help them grow their business, and I remember one eventful day of strategic planning where we started the day with ten people on the management team and ended with half that number. At 8:00 a.m., we began talking about how, in order to grow the business, the company needed to have a management team that was smaller—so they could be more nimble. At 10:00 a.m., we took a break and per the CEO's tough decision, five people packed up their stuff and left the executive leadership team then and there. These individuals stayed at the company, but it was a tectonic move.

It was a symbolic moment and it showed the importance of rightsizing your leadership team so your company can take things to the next level. Sometimes it takes a dramatic event like cutting your leadership team in half to see things clearly. In this case, it took having an offsite strategic planning day to allow us to look at the big picture and make some of these major adjustments.

Quarterly strategic planning meetings serve as a catalyst for change in a growing company.

RECESSION READINESS ASSESSMENT QUESTION #4

Does your company have a written, long-term, focused, strategic plan and do you spend at least one day each quarter updating it?

Does your leadership team spend at least one day each quarter on strategic planning, including updating your recession plan and doing a gap analysis of the talent, products, services, and geographical presence you lack? If so, score yourself GREEN.

We encourage you to conduct quarterly offsite meetings to work on your strategic plan and to use an outside consultant or facilitator to help plan and execute the meetings—and hold you accountable.

Why is it so important to have a consultant or facilitator? Without an experienced hand there to help guide the process, what inevitably happens is that the CEO or COO ends up running the strategic planning meeting themselves—and isn't able to fully participate. That's a mistake. Why would you want one of *the most important voices in the room* worrying about making sure everybody else participates rather than being fully engaged in thinking through the matters at hand and actually contributing to the work that's being done?

Your entire leadership team needs to be there. Spend a full day with them doing team building, culture work, and messaging to keep reiterating your core values. Talk about your strategic initiatives. Share high-level financials. Have select individuals and teams present what they're working on and highlight some of those key contributors on a rotating basis, so when the meeting is over, everybody understands the main goals for the quarter—and their roles in achieving those goals.

As you begin this journey, you may be missing key elements of strategic planning, like a gap analysis of the areas where you are lacking. If this sounds like you, score yourself YELLOW. Take the opportunity at your offsite meeting to analyze these areas and fill in the gaps.

If you're an entrepreneur who started your business out of your house and have never been coached or mentored, you may not have the business acumen to know what you don't know. If you're not doing quarterly strategic planning, score yourself RED. Even if you're very strong technically, think seriously about hiring an expert to help guide you through the process of strategic planning. It will make all the difference in terms of growing your business.

TAKING ACTION

Gather the list of materials recommended in this book and the *Rock the Recession* workbook and have your entire team take the Recession Readiness Assessment at www.recession.com/ready.

CHAPTER TWO

2ND GEAR—TUNE

Instructions for using **The Recession Gearbox:**

- 1st Gear (Assess) Always start with 1st Gear
- Then engage 2nd Gear (Tune), 3rd Gear (Race), and/or 4th Gear (Accelerate) depending on "The Economy"
    - If the Economy is in the Expansion or Recovery stages of the cycle, engage 2nd Gear, then 3rd Gear, then 4th Gear
    - If the Economy is in Recovery or Contraction, engage 3rd Gear, then 4th Gear
    - If the Economy is in Contraction or Recession, engage 4th Gear immediately if possible
- Use the Emergency Brake at any point if needed

And, above all else, use your judgment to determine which Gear to use given the circumstances within your company and outside in The Economy

PAUL: HOW I GOT MY HOUSE IN ORDER BEFORE THE RECESSION

In the year leading up to the Great Recession, I made sure—as part of our recession plan—to talk to my banker about increasing our line of credit. The point was to do it sooner rather than later. I also negotiated to eliminate our personal guarantees and improve our debt covenants. These were just some of the ways I sought to get our house in order *before* the downturn happened. I did this so that we could be better equipped to survive a recession and be in a position to *expand* during the recession.

Most people don't think this way. They wait until they *need* their banker, until they *need* their credit line increased— and by then it's too late. You simply can't do these things in a recession. It's a sad truth that when you need money the most, nobody wants to give you a loan. In a recession, banks won't normally extend your credit or reduce your personal guarantees or collateral obligations.

> The best time to ask your bank for a loan, or your investors, is when economic times are good.

Banks are hungry for business when the economy is doing well. They're fighting for clients. They're offering better deals. They *want* your business. Think of banking like any other strategic purchase and conduct a request for proposal (RFP) to get the best deal with a bank that can grow with your company.

The point is to do it all on a proactive basis. **Build up your flexibility now so when a recession happens, you can**

pounce. This is true whether it's a larger economic recession or just one of your competitors going into recession. Take advantage of the fact that most companies are not acting. They're stuck in *Groundhog Day*—doing the same thing over and over—trying to just keep up with the daily whirlwind and not thinking about obtaining additional borrowing capacity or lowering their financial risk.

They're coasting along with the top down (not prepared for a freak thunderstorm), totally exposed.

But the smart leaders know the peak of a recovery is the optimal time to tighten up their business and personal affairs—not only as a way of limiting the damage in a recession, but also to gear themselves up to take advantage of opportunities.

Take, for example, Rob Strobel of Lithko Contracting, a commercial, middle-market concrete contractor. He didn't wait for a recession to get his house in order. He saw a downturn coming, so he did things like lowering his pricing and aligning with key customers to take on strategic backlog. This foresight allowed him to win new work that carried him through the depths of the recession and gave him the ability to continue to grow. Squirrels have a biological imperative to gather nuts for winter; leaders don't. Unless you pay attention and take action, your company will starve.

Rob has it right when he says, "There are lots of folks in this industry who don't want to double down or take economic risks, so they don't lean into investments in the downturn. Instead of looking at how they can invest to gain market share, they look at how they can cut back. It's a mistake because when the market comes back, and now you have additional market share, you can rise *with* the market and see considerable growth."

Rob's numbers speak for themselves. Since coming out of the recession in 2011, Lithko has seen more than 20 percent compound annual growth. No surprise that when asked how he is feeling about the next recession, Rob responded with this: "It can't get here fast enough."

What about you? Are you going to be like me and Rob, or are you going to be like everyone else? The good news is you are already well on your way to recession readiness just by reading this book. In 1st Gear, you *assessed*. You benchmarked your own readiness compared to others, saw where you stood versus everybody else, and came to the conclusion that you need a plan—to be prepared for recessions both external and internal.

Now, in 2nd Gear, it's time to put pen to paper.

STRESS TESTING YOUR RECESSION READINESS

To make sure you have what it takes to weather a downturn, you need to stress test your company in a number of different ways. Each one of these stress tests is important, and they all work in conjunction with one another. Skip a test at your own peril!

ZIPPER YOUR RELATIONSHIPS

As Mike Lancaster, from Frank L. Blum Construction, puts it: "Are your customer and vendor relationships 'zippered' from top to bottom?" One big mistake people make is they only have one contact at each company they work with. The problem, of course, is that in a recession your contact may get fired, and then you'll be starting from scratch! You always need to know your contact's boss, as well as the other people who work for that same boss. The last thing you want is to suddenly have to call the boss out of the blue after your primary contact gets let go.

In order to know which relationships merit zippering, you need to know who your top vendors and clients are and how that list has evolved over time. Who are they this year and who were they last year? What differences do you see between this year's and last year's lists? What surprises?

Are any of your top clients at risk during a recession due

to their particular industry? Do any of them represent 10 percent or more of your revenue?

Remember, **losing one big client can put your company in a recession.** That is why it's so important to be vigilant—even obsessive compulsive—about collecting receivables from your largest customers and that you really understand what their financial condition is at all times. As we've learned, recessions tend to expose those companies that have been "swimming naked." Ask for regular updates from your clients on their pipeline of work and what they're experiencing in the market and assess the risk of project delays or late payment due to a slowdown of their business. When you engage your clients in these discussions, you will be viewed as more of a business partner than a vendor. So, don't be afraid to have these conversations.

If you want to pounce, you can't leave your underbelly exposed! Make sure your top clients are secure and you're on top of collecting money you're owed.

Make sure to ask yourself: what is the quality and depth of my relationship with each client?

A 2013 article by Nickell, Rollins, and Hellman emphasizes the importance of relationships in surviving and thriving in a recession: "Partnering with key customers to work together during down times appears to be the most critical [factor] to success."

But shouldn't you treat all your customers equally? To put it bluntly: no. In his book *The Pumpkin Plan*, Mike Michalowicz encourages readers to always *prioritize the stars.* "When the good ones call," he writes, "they get serviced first. The cringe-worthy clients get pushed to the back of the line...The cringers will get the hint. Sure it's a little bit *Mean Girls*, but it gets the job done."

RECESSION READINESS
ASSESSMENT QUESTION #5

Does your company's leadership team understand the financial health of its major customers and vendors?

This means taking your top twenty customers, putting them into market segments, and analyzing those segments in terms of how a recession would impact them. You may find, for example, that you have an overconcentration in the retail industry. But, upon further segmenting retail, you understand that not all retail is created equal. In fact, **some retail customers—like Walmart or Dollar General—actually tend to do better in a recession.** The high-end retailers, like Tiffany & Co. and Saks, tend to stumble.

Companies that score GREEN on this question will use this analysis to go out and diversify their customer base and grow recession-resistant market segments. They will meet with their top twenty customers quarterly to assess their financial health. If you do this, it will help keep you close to your customer, close to reality—and allow you to deal with facts on the ground regarding your customer service, your products, and your competitiveness.

Talking to your customers about what their plans are for a recession and how they view it gives you good knowledge about whether they're looking to expand and take advantage of a recession or whether they're planning to just hunker down.

When you know a customer is going to hide in their shell like a turtle and just try to survive, **you need to come up with cost-saving ideas to remain a relevant value-added business partner.** The point is that if you *know* in advance that your customers are going to behave like turtles, you can be proactive and come up with cost-saving ideas *for* them—ideas that allow you to be part of their plan instead of just part of their cuts!

Another example of green on question #5 comes from a seventy-four-year-old sushi master from Kyubey restaurant in the Ginza district of Tokyo. Yosuke Imada is the owner of the restaurant and on a recent visit, he came over to greet Jonathan's family personally. In an interview published in the *Wall Street Journal* in 2007, Imada said that when the Japanese economy crashed in 1989, his restaurant was okay because they hadn't overextended themselves before the recession. He continues that "everyone's money is the same" and advises that regular customers won't be around forever, so it is important to treat all patrons equally. What impressed Jonathan most is that Imada is still "walking the talk" of his own advice over a decade later. If you're ever in Tokyo, make the pilgrimage to Kyubey restaurant for some excellent sushi. It's expensive, but you get a "free" lesson in how to be green on how to cultivate strong relationships with your customers with every meal.

Conversely, if you know your customers are planning to pounce during a recession and acquire other companies or assets, having this knowledge in advance will allow you to proactively plan to support their growth.

If you're already doing this stuff, great—you're green. Stay with it! But if you're like Jonathan was with Fitness Together, you should score yourself YELLOW. At his personal training studios, Jonathan had clients start every one-hour session with fifteen minutes on the treadmill, which was a great way to find out how they were feeling. Often, they would vent their misgivings about the economy and give some interesting insights. But that was the extent of it. Jonathan and his team didn't do anything with that information. They had a good finger on the pulse of the economy just by talking to their customers individually and hearing their stories. In particular, they learned about different frustrations in different locations. Once the recession hit, they understood that if they were going to have to close locations, it made more sense to close the ones in less affluent communities. In the more affluent neighborhoods, they knew from talking to their customers that the recession would only cost them money on paper, but wouldn't really affect their buying decision when it came to their health and wellness.

So if you're like Jonathan was and you have a yellow score, keep talking to your customers. And start to create more of a discipline around these conversations, as well as a plan to act on the information you are gathering.

Now, if you're not currently talking to your customers and vendors in any organized way at all, you get a RED score here. It's not just a matter of getting started; you need to shift your whole way of thinking. **As a top leader of your organization, it's up to you to lead from the front.** If you haven't done that and it's not in your culture, that's a heavy lift. You need to make a big change and start having your leadership team go out and meet with customers and vendors face-to-face. The kind of information we're after doesn't come out in email surveys nor in quick phone calls.

I can't stress this enough: talking to customers is critical in building long-term relationships, because it means you're having open and honest conversations with your key customers, your top 20 percent (who often make up 50 to 80 percent of your revenue!). If you can zipper these relationships, you'll be in good shape.

> Are your customer and vendor relationships "zippered" from top to bottom?

STRESS TESTING YOUR VENDORS

In the same way recession-ready companies stay in touch with their customers, you need to also meet regularly with your key *vendors* to stress test them in an organized fashion. Don Greenland's company, that we met earlier, is a great example of this discipline. Not only does the company, Nabholz, have a very strong recession plan, it also pays unique attention to pre-qualification of vendors and their ongoing health.

Stress testing your vendors—putting in place a pre-qualification process for them and subcontractors—is a great way to make sure projects and inventory don't go off track as your company grows.

Paul and his team at Roth certainly dealt with lots of national and international vendors and suppliers, but they didn't regularly stress test them. Their ad hoc meetings with vendors were valuable nonetheless. They learned how their suppliers' new technology benefitted Roth's customers. There was an exchange of open and honest feedback on both sides, with the goal of bringing customers the newest innovations for the best prices. But there wasn't an explicit process at Roth for stress testing.

It's a lot easier to get this discipline right if you have people on your leadership team, and people at your vendors and suppliers, who have actually been through a recession before. What's most important is for you to build up critical awareness you've been missing about your vendors' and suppliers' needs. If you don't understand what they need, you can't take advantage of the opportunities a recession may present, like the ability to negotiate lower prices for equipment and supplies.

RECESSION READINESS
ASSESSMENT QUESTION #6

Is your company's EBITDA margin "best in class" for your industry?

When you experience substantial growth in all areas of your business, you can grow right through a recession. If you are GREEN on question #6, it means you have a strong EBITDA margin—shoot for 10 percent or better—and are well positioned to continue looking for new growth opportunities within and outside of your customer base.

At Roth, for example, because it was a high-margin business, Paul and his team were able to reinvest in the latest technology. They had eighteen people in their IT department, which is highly unusual for a contractor. They did a lot of their own programming to enhance customer experience and reduce operational inefficiencies. If you have a strong EBITDA margin, you need to take advantage of your cash flow to develop specialized, proprietary products and services because of the value this intellectual property drives.

But if your EBITDA margin is not quite there—if it's *approaching* best in class for companies in your industry but not at that level—score yourself a YELLOW here. Go back to benchmarking yourself versus your competitors and ensure you understand the levers you need to pull to increase or maximize the value of your business. Then focus on strategies to grow either unique, one-off, niche-project businesses or more general, annuity service businesses.

If your EBITDA is not best in class, and not even approaching that level, then score yourself RED. It's time for you to do a full review of all aspects of your business. Pay attention to and eliminate non-revenue-generating employees and strategies. Benchmark your company and learn about the levers that will increase and maximize the value of your business and then start to pull them!

RECESSION READINESS ASSESSMENT QUESTION #7

Does your company have 5 to 10 percent of its next twelve months of estimated revenue as equity on your balance sheet?

If you don't understand Recession Readiness Assessment question #7 or the explanation, invest in your own personal financial growth!

Our *balance sheet stress test* shows whether you have enough equity (5 to 10 percent or more of your next twelve months of estimated revenue) to survive a recession. If you have an equity shortfall (less than 5 to 10 percent of your next twelve months of estimated revenue as equity on your balance sheet), what steps can you take to meet your target threshold? For example, you might consider curbing all non-tax distributions, working to increase your profit margin, or cutting costs to reduce overhead.

Research shows that the size of your company and its balance sheet *does* matter when it comes to surviving a recession; bigger is better. The same goes for how long your company has been around—the longer your company's history, the harder it is for it to be brought down by a recession. But the biggest factor here, according to CJ Rhoads, is how much money your company has *retained* from its earnings over the years. The more you've saved for a rainy day, the more likely you are to thrive during a recession.

Different industries have different benchmarks, but the common denominator is that the more labor you have, the closer to 10 percent in equity on the balance sheet you're going to need to be in relation to your next twelve months of revenue. For example, say you're a $20 million contractor that's also a subcontractor that supplies labor, and your forecast for the following year shows you moving to about $30 million of volume. In this scenario, you will need $3 million of equity—10 percent times

$30 million—to provide the necessary working capital (without over-leveraging your company) to support that growth. If, on the other hand, you're a general contractor who does no self performance (provides no jobsite labor), 5 percent in balance sheet equity is okay because you don't have weekly payroll going out the door.

Here is a hard truth: **most business leaders don't understand their financial statements.** They don't take the time to understand what working capital is and what level of liquidity (cash or credit) they need to fund and support their growth.

Don't let this be you. Act now to improve your financial literacy. The strength of your balance sheet is a critical measurement, and if you don't understand it, you can't use it to grow.

> "Running your business off of the income statement is like high school math, running your business off of the balance sheet is like college accounting, and running your business off the cash-flow statement is like having your doctorate in finance."—Paul Belair

If you understand your balance sheet and how to use it to support growth, score yourself GREEN on question #7. Your balance sheet is strong, and you should be having regular conversations with your accountant to discuss advanced tax avoidance strategies to maximize your company's value and your net worth.

If you're *not* proactively in discussions with your financial partners and advisors, chances are your awareness is limited and you need to score yourself YELLOW. The first step is to start looking at your banker as a business partner.

If you're yellow, you probably also haven't accurately forecasted your line of credit and cash needs for the next twelve months. Meet with your banker and forecast outgoing cash flow for the next four quarters to understand your cash needs. If analysis shows you're going to max out your line of credit in the second quarter, you need to ask your bank *now* for an extension to your credit line. Your bank will work with you; however, you have to proactively go to them and demonstrate you're growing and profitable and have a plan to succeed.

And what if you're not growing at all? If you're like Jonathan was with Fitness Together, you have negative equity on your balance sheet, meaning there are more liabilities than assets. Unfortunately, this was common throughout Jonathan's time with that business. It meant there was no room for growth. When things started to slow down with the recession, options were limited to either closing one or more of their five studios or selling studios to one of their managers or employees (to take over the unit and its liability).

If this sounds like you, if your balance sheet is weak, score yourself RED on this question. It's not the end of the world, but it does demand immediate attention. You have to be honest with yourself and set a FAST (Finite, Attainable, Specific, and Timely) goal for improving your balance sheet. It's not going to happen overnight, but step-by-step you'll get there.

Be courageous and discuss your situation with your banker to find solutions together. And be vulnerable enough to admit to yourself that a weak balance sheet isn't a character flaw—but left unchecked, it's a major business issue.

> Left unchecked, a weak balance sheet will bring your company down in a recession.

RECESSION READINESS
ASSESSMENT QUESTION #8

Does your company's leadership team regularly meet with its bank representatives to discuss the company's line of credit to ensure the limit is right for current and future business needs?

If you scored yourself GREEN on question #8, it means that you are treating your banker the way you should—as a strategic business partner. You're keeping them informed on where you're going, where you are, and where you have been. There are no surprises because you're always proactively discussing the business with them.

Unfortunately, most companies don't act this way. They treat their banker like their dentist, like someone they see, begrudgingly, twice a year—and only because they *have* to go. If that sounds like your relationship with your banker, score yourself a YELLOW here. You need to understand you're only hurting yourself: **keeping your banker out of the loop is a self-defeating proposition**. It may seem counterintuitive, but maintaining this important relationship will lower your anxiety when times get tough.

We can't stress it enough: **know your banker.** Be aware of your debt covenants and test them quarterly on a rolling twelve months' basis. Be aware of what the next six months' projections are so you can proactively discuss them with your banker and get on the same page about where your business is going.

If you're not having these conversations with your banker at all—conversations to rightsize your credit limit—score yourself a RED here. If you don't change this pattern, you'll soon find your relationship in jeopardy. Keep yourself out of a situation where your banker tells you that you violated a covenant and you're not even aware of it. There's no good outcome for you in that scenario.

On a positive note, take comfort in the fact that bankers are actually people and have discretion. Work to establish a real relationship with your banker that goes beyond surface conversation. Meet them regularly for coffee or a meal. Show them you care about the relationship. Go ahead, do it now. Schedule a call or meeting with your banker. Remember: the best time to ask for a loan is when you don't need one.

> Your banker wants you to be successful, needs you to be successful, and will help you get into the right financial products to support your growth. Work on this relationship before the recession and it will pay dividends.

YOUR LINE OF CREDIT

How do you know whether you have enough line of credit (LOC) availability to allow you to capitalize on opportunities during the recession, like purchasing assets and other companies? How do you know whether you have enough LOC availability to weather the storm of a recession?

First, ask yourself, was there a time over the past twelve months where you could reduce your line of credit to zero for thirty days or more and not have any credit outstanding (if for no other reason than to demonstrate financial strength)? The reason this ability to pay off your LOC is important is that most business leaders, especially those of companies under $100 million, don't understand cash flow and particularly the significance of the cash flow statement.

The cash flow statement shows that—if you're growing—you increasingly have your cash tied up in receivables. If you can stay on top of this information, you can take strategic action, on a proactive basis, to extend the accounts payable terms with your suppliers and subcontractors to better match your collection terms.

Paul did exactly this at Roth. Because the company's business was seasonal, work would ramp up in April (after a slow season from December to March), and they'd have payroll flying out the door in the summer months. If he and his team hadn't been on top of it, they would have bumped up against their line of credit limit. Because they were proactive, they carefully managed accounts payable and rigorously collected accounts receivable to control their cash flow.

As you've probably experienced yourself, when you are proactive in this way, vendors are much more accommodating. It's a lot better than what happens to a lot of companies, where they don't pay their vendors on time and then get *the call* telling them they're being put on a credit hold. In order to avoid this fate, you have to be self-aware and understand the levers that impact your cash flow.

Now, what if you *weren't* able to get out of your line of credit (pay it down to zero) for at least three of the last twelve months? If this is your reality, you must understand, first of all, that you have the wrong banking product for your needs. You are using your line of credit as if it were term debt. A line of credit is supposed to be tied to your working capital, which is tied to your receivables. If you have a line of credit that you don't exit for more than ninety days, you are using your line of credit as long-term debt rather than short-term debt. This is bad news: you risk violating a bank covenant and going into the "workout group" at the bank, plus you're probably paying a higher interest rate than you should be.

> "Workout" bankers are the ones who take over companies that violate their debt covenants and show an inability to "get it." They sell assets or make decisions to mitigate the bank's exposure, often to the severe detriment of the business.

If this is you, meet with your accountant and your banker. Discuss a bridge plan to get from where you are now to a place where you can use your line of credit (or other short-term debt vehicles) appropriately. This bridge plan may involve terming out all or part of your line of credit and not letting yourself make the same mistake again. This is a good thing: smaller companies often don't have the ability to get off of their line of credit or credit cards. This was certainly the case with Jonathan and Fitness Together: they never had any extra cash available because they used their line like it was term debt. Their initial SBA loan didn't include enough room for working capital to support their growth, a big mistake.

And **remember to stay in touch with your banker**. Why is this so important? Your banker can provide very valuable financing. Without it, you have to raise money from investors or put more of your own cash in to fund the business's growth.

RECESSION READINESS
ASSESSMENT QUESTION #9

Does your company's leadership team know all restrictions in place on any company debt and do they review these "covenants" monthly to ensure compliance?

A debt covenant is a fancy way of saying an agreement

you've made with your bank or lender. These covenants are found in your loan agreement. The **debt covenant stress test** shows how much cushion you have before you trip your covenants. At what earnings level would you violate any of your covenants?

If you scored yourself GREEN on this question, it means you're a savvy company, you've read and understand the debt covenants in your loan agreement, and you measure against them to ensure compliance on a regular basis. Sadly, the majority of people at the ownership level of a company don't know what a net worth covenant or a debt service covenant ratio is. They don't know how close they are to failing their covenants, and they don't measure them.

NOW, THEREFORE, THE PARTIES COVENANT AND AGREE AS FOLLOWS:

1. The following financial covenants contained in the Agreement shall be amended as follows:

- Line is to be monitored with a monthly Borrowing Base Report and Accounts Receivable Aging. The Borrowing Base Report to be defined as follows: Accounts Receivable less ineligible Accounts Receivable advanced at 75%. Ineligible Accounts Receivable is to include Accounts Receivable over 90 days from due date and all Work In Process. Borrowing Base Report is to be supported by Accounts Receivable aging report.

- Monthly Borrowing Base Reports supported by Monthly Accounts Receivable, Accounts Payable Agings as well as work in process report.

- Debt Service Coverage Ratio. Maintain a Debt Service Coverage Ratio that does not fall below 1.15 beginning 12/31/12. The Debt Service Coverage Ratio will be evaluated for each annual statement. The term "Debt Service Coverage Ratio", expressed as a mathematical formula, means (Net Income + Depreciation Expense + Amortization Expense + Interest Expense)/ (Current Portion Long Term Debt 4- Interest Expense + Other Interest Expense + Dividends/ Distributions + Non-Financed Capital Expenditures).

If you're green on this question, it means you're highly proactive and aware. You're on top of your numbers. If you see you're going to miss a number, you know it ahead of time. Like Paul, you have the CFO or controller of your company prepare a monthly or quarterly one-page summary of your debt covenants and your company's cushion with regard to each covenant, so you always keep this important information at the forefront.

But what if you're aware of your covenants but don't know exactly where your business stands? In that case, you should score yourself YELLOW. You get points for being aware, but you haven't proactively forecasted or dealt with your banker ahead of time. You need to know your company's numbers and educate your banker as to the business conditions that led to that result, and what you are proactively doing to handle your situation. This best practice will give you credibility with your banker so they're not surprised. As we've learned, the worst thing is for your banker to be surprised: when that happens, they take your bad news to their boss or the credit committee within the bank—and you damage your reputation.

> Just like you wouldn't want to be shocked or surprised by your customer, you don't want to startle your banker.

If you're like Jonathan was when he was with Fitness Together, you have some debt covenants but don't know exactly what they are. If this sounds like you, score yourself a RED here. Fitness Together was a small business with an SBA loan, which included several debt covenants.

One covenant that Jonathan *did* know about was his promise not to sell $50,000 in a stock portfolio that was collateral for their loan. He sold that stock portfolio before finishing paying off the loan, which was actually a violation of the debt covenant. He didn't really think about it at the time because he wasn't regularly reviewing and testing the company's covenants. Luckily, it happened right before the company's final SBA payment in the last year of the loan. Otherwise, they might have had to go through an audit or worse.

Don't be negligent with your loan. If you are, you'll put your loan officer in a bad situation. They'll lose time defending you to a credit committee. Remember, your banker is a human being with a job to do and a reputation. The more time they spend focused on fixing your loan, the less time they have to source and grant new loans, which is how they earn a living. Don't put them in that situation.

RECESSION READINESS
ASSESSMENT QUESTION #10

Do your company's owners regularly review any personal guarantees on company debt and are they actively working to reduce them to zero?

For the **personal guarantee stress test**, make a list of any personal guarantees you may have with your bank or bonding company.

> NOTICE: FOR THIS NOTICE "YOU" MEANS THE GUARANTOR AND "CREDITOR" AND "HIS" MEANS LENDER
> **WARNING - BY SIGNING THIS PAPER YOU GIVE UP YOUR RIGHT TO NOTICE AND COURT TRIAL. IF YOU DO NOT PAY ON TIME A COURT JUDGMENT MAY BE TAKEN AGAINST YOU WITHOUT YOUR PRIOR KNOWLEDGE AND THE POWERS OF A COURT CAN BE USED TO COLLECT FROM YOU REGARDLESS OF ANY CLAIMS YOU MAY HAVE AGAINST THE CREDITOR WHETHER FOR RETUNRED GOODS, FAULTY GOODS, FAILURE ON HIS PART TO COMPLY WITH THE AGREEMENT, OR ANY OTHER CAUSE.**

If you're GREEN on personal guarantees, it means you've actively reduced your guarantees or capped them.

It is not unusual to sign for debt; people give personal guarantees to banks as well as surety bonding companies. Your goal, however, is to reduce your personal guarantees down to a non-existent level or a minimal amount of your overall wealth.

If this sounds like you—if you are actively striving to reduce your personal guarantees—score yourself a YELLOW here. When the economy is booming, that's a great time to ask your bank if they'll reduce your personal guarantees, waive them altogether, or put a cap on them. Usually, the only way to get out of a personal guarantee entirely is to switch banks[2]. It takes growth and strong

---

2   With SBA loans, there is no getting out of the personal guarantee. You can usually only get out of a personal guarantee with commercial bank loans not backed by the SBA.

financial ratios to earn your bank's flexibility with guarantees. But if the economy is in recovery (growth) mode, there are going to be banks that want your business.

> A strong economic environment is almost always the best time to negotiate reductions in your personal guarantees.

If, however, you are not working to reduce your personal guarantees or your bank has already called in a personal guarantee, that puts you in a different situation. If that has happened to you, score yourself a RED here. It means your personal assets are at risk of repossession. Even if you leave your business, until that guarantee is paid off, you are still responsible—which is why you always have to be very careful when signing a personal guarantee.

RECESSION READINESS
ASSESSMENT QUESTION #11

Does your company have cash or debt available to fund growth?

This **liquidity stress test** asks the simple question: how much liquid cash does your company and its owners have available? This may seem unrelated to the project of stress testing your company's recession readiness. Maybe—maybe not. Let's say you have an opportunity during a recession to buy a competitor, but the bank won't lend you the money. If you had, say, $3 million of your own money available, you could potentially put that cash back into the company and buy the competitor. Obviously, this isn't always a smart move. But sometimes it's worth it to take advantage of a once-in-a-lifetime opportunity to pounce during a recession.

Of course, in order to pounce on these kinds of opportunities—to acquire talent, acquire equipment or supplies, or acquire companies in areas where you're looking to grow—you have to have adequate liquidity. If this sounds like you, score yourself GREEN here, and focus on making sure your company doesn't fall out of green on this crucial question.

What if you're not 100 percent sure? What if you feel like it might be too risky to wager part of your personal net worth or to take on extra debt for expansion? In this case, score yourself YELLOW. Develop a tighter acquisition target list and re-examine why you want to grow. You need conviction to buy a company or assets during bad times.

Now, if your debt is already high and you don't have the capacity to take on more for expansion, that means you are RED on this question. You might be able to scrape enough cash together to make some moves, but overall you're going to lose out on opportunities to acquire new equipment and supplies from companies going out of business in a recession. The only way to capitalize on others' mistakes in the next downturn is to start developing a war chest of savings to tap so you can be nimble enough to make better, more financially sensible moves.

Think about what having a war chest might look and feel like! Think about your largest competitor—the one that keeps nipping at your clients or trying to steal your employees. Maybe they're a perfect, complementary business you could buy if and when they hit hard times? Your biggest competitor could be a perfect acquisition target for you. But will you have the means to afford it?

RECESSION READINESS ASSESSMENT QUESTION #12

Does your company have a board of advisors that meets at least quarterly with the leadership team to help set plans for growth, ask challenging questions, and hold the team accountable for its action plans?

If you score yourself GREEN on this question, it means that you have outside accountability for your leadership team. This outside group of advisors or board looks at all aspects of your business and helps you gain knowledge about your strategies, budgets, cash flow, and forecasts.

A lot of companies dabble with a board of advisors, but don't meet regularly. Or they just meet with their accountant and their lawyer. If that's the case with you, score yourself YELLOW here. The problem with just meeting with your accountant or lawyer—who you pay on an hourly basis—is that you're probably not getting the hard-hitting advice and counsel you need.

Instead of relying on your professional advisors, **assemble your own group of people who possess the specific talents you're missing yourself or lacking on your team.** Having an advisory board of experts will bring tremendous value to your company. And while you're at it, why not try to find advisors who have experience navigating recessions?

Understand that you can have a board of advisors at any level of the company. For example, if you're the head of sales for your company, you can assemble a board to give you feedback. It's not just the owner or CEO of a business that can benefit from regularly meeting with experts.

If you are scoring yellow on question #12, consider **joining a group like the Young Presidents' Organization (YPO), the Entrepreneurs' Organization (EO), or**

Vistage. These organizations will provide you with a forum where you're paired with six to eight other members who hold one another accountable. Without this accountability, you can easily wind up missing something or writing something off as noncritical because you don't have the appropriate perspective.

If you *don't* have a board of advisors and you're not in any groups like YPO or EO, you should score yourself RED on this question. At the very least, you can start by engaging a paid mentor or executive coach. This person will keep you in check, tell it like it is, and help you see where you need to improve in running your business. Hiring a great coach means doing your homework. Speak with their references and confirm their accomplishments.

DEVELOP YOUR PIT CREW (BOARD OF ADVISORS)

A board of advisors will serve as your "Pit Crew" before, during, and after a recession. As a leader of your company, you need a Pit Crew that will hold you accountable for executing your recession plan—and tell you when you're driving the business dangerously close to a fiery crash!

> Your Pit Crew will serve as a sounding board for you, create a broader network, and help you see around corners.

Who *should* be in your Pit Crew? You want people who are *smarter* than you and who have proven track records. Most importantly, these people need to be willing to call you out! Seek advisors who are true experts and who have already achieved a high level of success. That will free them up to give you some real, hard-hitting feedback. Last, but not least, try to have at least one person on your board who has been through a recession and hopefully grown through it. The point is that it's not just about having an advisory board—you have to have the *right* people on the board.

Who should you steer clear of having on your board of advisors? You definitely *don't* want your Pit Crew to be made up of friends and family, nor do you want your management team on the board. Even professionals like your banker, lawyer, or accountant are a bad idea. Yes, they want and need you to be successful, but they may not always be totally honest with you—out of fear they'll upset the relationship and you'll fire them.

You want advisors who have no ulterior motives, no other reason for serving on the board than paying it forward and being a good mentor or steward. People like that can really tell you if you're being stupid or heading for a crash. And you'll need that tough talk from time to time, believe us! A good Pit Crew will always keep you honest and accountable. Accountability, in turn, will increase your performance and up your game.

We recommend meeting with your Pit Crew quarterly for a half day. You should send them materials to review in advance (e.g., company financials, strategy roadmaps). Each Pit Crew member should receive between $500 and $2,500 per meeting depending on the size of your company and the scope of their commitment.

YOUR FINANCIAL TEAM

Like with your Pit Crew, you need to pay attention to make sure you have the right accountant, banker, and insurance firm (and the right bonding company if you're a contractor). Take stock of your situation and rightsize your advisors on an annual basis. You want financial partners who have the capacity to grow with you. To maximize growth, consider switching to a regional firm once you reach $10 to 25 million in revenue because you're going to want more sophisticated advice and to leverage their relationships and contacts, and you may even end up hiring some of their employees to come to work for you. (Don't actively poach from your advisors, but often people will want to leave professional careers to come "in-house" with a favorite client—and this is a good way to meet those potential candidates.)

On the accounting side, as your company grows, switch to a larger firm that adds value because they have more subject matter expertise in your industry. But choose carefully: you don't usually want to be the biggest client of the firm if you're a high-growth company. Work with advisors who can help you understand the least risky path to take your company to the next level and who work with many clients in your industry who are larger than you.

You need to re-evaluate your partners and advisors as your company grows. If you're like a lot of companies, you have *some* strong relationships, but not with all your financial partners. Keep in mind that **you should not have the same advisors when you're at $15 million in revenue as when you were $5 million in size**. You may feel guilty letting them go, but it's good business hygiene. And they should want you to work with new professionals that can support your growth!

> The advisors who got you to where you are now aren't necessarily the professionals who are going to get you to where you want to go.

The accountants at a mid-size firm may be more expensive, but they can make introductions in banking, have vast industry experience you can leverage, and can save you money on taxes. They have the resources to stay on top of their game.

At Fitness Together, Jonathan's accountant was a sole proprietor focused on restaurants, not fitness centers.

He was used to dealing with cash businesses, but in the personal training business people collect prepayment up front from their clients—for ten, twenty-five, fifty, one hundred personal training sessions—and then they "owe" the clients those sessions until the clients use them. It is important not to spend the prepayments until the client uses the sessions they are owed. If Jonathan had selected the right accountant—an industry specialist or at least someone more familiar with fitness providers (rather than restaurants)—that advisor could have given him more guidance much earlier about the importance of matching revenue (prepayments) with direct expenses (sessions owed to clients). It wasn't the accountant's fault the relationship was a bad match.

TAKING ACTION

Now that you understand the importance of getting your house in order *before* a recession, it's time for you to take action—to go out and have the conversations you need to have with your banker, your financial advisor, your accountant, your insurance agent, and your lawyer.

Whenever we talk about the importance of 2nd Gear, about having these conversations when the economy is strong, the reaction we tend to get is people slapping their foreheads, saying things like, "I wish I had thought of that!"

Don't be like them. Make a commitment right now and actually schedule these meetings before it's too late. Here's what that looks like:

- Now that you are committed to talking to your banker about increasing your line of credit—or about lowering your personal guarantees so you've got less risk—*when* are you going to have that meeting? Schedule a date.
- *When* are you going to meet with your financial advisor? Schedule a date.
- *When* are you going to meet with your accountant? Schedule a date.
- *When* are you going to meet with your insurance agent? Schedule a date.
- *When* are you going to meet with your lawyer? Schedule a date.
- Remember: getting your house in order, getting your key customer list zippered, getting your balance sheet strong, getting your line of credit increased, getting your personal guarantees reduced—these actions aren't only important in terms of taking your business to the next level during a recession. They're also just good business hygiene (business best practices).

CHAPTER THREE

3RD GEAR—RACE

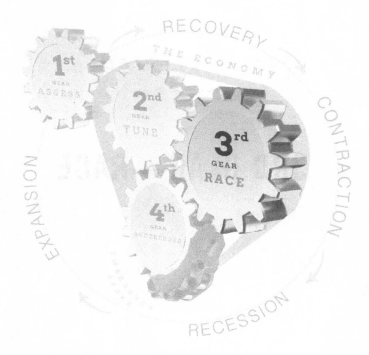

Instructions for using **The Recession Gearbox:**

⚙ 1st Gear (Assess) Always start with 1st Gear

⚙ Then engage 2nd Gear (Tune), 3rd Gear (Race), and/or 4th Gear (Accelerate) depending on "The Economy"

- If the Economy is in the Expansion or Recovery stages of the cycle, engage 2nd Gear, then 3rd Gear, then 4th Gear
- If the Economy is in Recovery or Contraction, engage 3rd Gear, then 4th Gear
- If the Economy is in Contraction or Recession, engage 4th Gear immediately if possible

🖐 Use the Emergency Brake at any point if needed

And, above all else, use your judgment to determine which Gear to use given the circumstances within your company and outside in The Economy

CAPITALIZING ON OPPORTUNITIES

When approaching a recession, you can slam on the brakes or you can stomp on the gas. What's your plan?

Everything you've learned so far is, of course, good strategic planning in general. But in a recession it becomes turbocharged. **Think of a recession as the fuel or accelerant.** Let it rip!

Especially if you're looking for an American Dream Exit, you *need* that boost to get to the bigger-sale opportunity. You need it if you're trying to 10X your business. Of course, it's technically possible (but unlikely) to grow your business exponentially at any juncture; the point is **recessions give you opportunities that might otherwise take a decade or more to bear fruit.**

The problem is recessions don't happen very often. Doesn't that statement sound strange? Strange and true: recessions are rare opportunities. That's *why* you're doing all this work. It's why you bought this book in the first place so you could put together a strategic plan to pounce—so you'll be ready. You know you can't just wait around, that you have to get serious about capitalizing on this moment.

Now the time has come, and you're right where you wanted to be.

While everyone else is waiting it out in the fetal position, you're investing. **Instead of being paralyzed by fear, you're taking advantage of others' lack of prepara-**

tion. Just like Warren Buffett did, when he made all that money bailing out GE Capital and Wells Fargo. Or like Southwest Airlines did during the 1990–1991 recession when they bought jets and acquired landing slots from a failed competitor.

> Recessions don't come around often. Seize the opportunity!

This is the gear where you *let it rip*—and take advantage of the fact that, unlike your competitors, you know when to floor it, when to tap the brakes, when to ride the draft, and when to shift gears. Because you've prepared, you won't be excessively cautious, taking things too slow. You won't be desperately aggressive, taking turns too fast. And you won't be overly eager and reckless, hitting the wall.

USING YOUR RECESSION ACQUISITION PLAN

As we've learned, recessions are a wonderful time to stock up on cheap assets, disruptive technologies, A-players (top employees), and competitors who didn't think to create a recession plan.

You should have a list of the competitors you've had your eye on to acquire in a recession. Now's the time to use that list—and jump on the opportunities you've identified. Remember, this will only work if you've already built these relationships.

Start having conversations with—and getting to know—your acquisition targets well before the recession happens. Obviously, you don't come right out and tell them you want to buy them! What you do is invest consistent time and energy to foster a good working relationship.

Remember, too, you're trying to fill specific gaps from your strategic plan. If you're a plumbing company, for example, you don't necessarily have to just foster relationships with *other plumbing companies*. Focus on the companies that will complement your existing organization and make it stronger in the ways you're not.

You want to keep your friends close and your enemies closer. That way you will know, when the time comes, which are the most desirable businesses to fulfill your recession acquisition plan. If it turns out that one or more of these companies have stumbled in the recession, you'll be waiting in the wings—and will already have a relationship with them, which will make integrating them into your company all that much easier.

Often, when people sell their businesses, they want to sell to people they know and trust. That's good news for you if your relationship has been well established far in advance of going into any negotiation.

> You shouldn't try to start a relationship to acquire a competitor when the economy is already crashing. They'll trust you far more if you establish a relationship before the downturn.

PAUL: POUNCING DOES NOT MEAN BETTING THE FARM

When the race is on and the recession is approaching, you're going to want to pounce. After all, this is what you've been planning all along. But that doesn't mean you won't make mistakes, which is why you should **never bet the farm**.

I made a classic mistake when we found a renewable, wind-powered energy startup opportunity to invest in—one that would benefit, if successful, every major division within Roth. It was a company located in Ohio, and their main product was an emerging technology to capture wind power on commercial rooftops. What made the product special was that it tied into companies' electrical systems to reduce their energy usage, and whenever it harvested more energy than what was being used by the facility, the excess power could be sold back to the grid for a net savings!

As part of their research and development, the startup

had engaged a NASA engineer, who specialized in wind energy, to fully test and certify the prototype. It was virtually guaranteed to work and was an ideal match for the products we sold at Roth. For example, in order to use the product, you had to put the structure on a commercial roof, which meant having to make penetrations in the roofing membrane. This was something not all companies were certified to do, but we were. Check√

Then there was metal fabrication for the frame that needed to be done, and Roth had its own large metal fabrication shop. Check√

Then, you had to know something about electricity and how to monitor energy usage. We had our own national energy management company and a monitoring company that would allow us to monitor each wind capturing unit 24/7. Check√

Wait—there was even more...The unit was so sophisticated that it turned in to the direction of the wind to increase the wind going through the funnel, creating what is called the Bernoulli Effect: as wind speed increases, so does the amount of power generation a wind turbine is capable of producing. This movement meant the unit required a high level of *service*. And, we just happened to have a national HVAC service business. Check√

You can see why I was excited about the wind startup opportunity: it fit like a glove into all our products and services, and this was all happening during a time when I was trying to break down walls between divisions at Roth. **I used to joke we were four different companies that just happened to show up to work at the same place.** My goal was to maximize overall results by having each division work effectively together.

We had just rebranded the company *Roth: Powered by Green* to take advantage of the high energy costs at the time, as well as the cost-reduction culture sweeping the country as everyone was trying to survive the Great Recession. Everyone was looking for cost-saving ideas. And our national retailers were looking for consumer-friendly, sustainable, green-energy branding. Everything was coming together nicely. As we started to pitch the wind startup, we had a lot of people signing up for pilot programs—and there was great excitement and buzz. It helped build our new brand throughout our national customer base.

Now, we just needed to get to a working prototype. But in order to do so, we had to invest $700,000. As we were reviewing this investment, one of my four partners at Roth brought up some objections. Instead of listening to what he had to say, I shut him down. I was just so convinced this was a magic elixir. I was so laser-focused on our new *Roth: Powered by Green* brand—and on pulling through more of our energy-saving products and services to our national customers—that I failed to explore my partner's objections.

After we made the investment and got to prototype day, we were invited to a board meeting at the startup. At the meeting, the owner showed up in a brand-new four-door Lexus with a personalized license plate. I knew then and there I was probably in trouble. He used our money to get a new car instead of investing in the product!

But, maybe not. The deal I had negotiated still had a lot going for it. The first installation of the prototype was being done by a very reputable customer of ours. As part of our investment, the startup agreed to give Roth sole sourcing on manufacturing (metal fabrication), roofing, servicing, energy management, and monitoring of the units. This deal meant we'd have a steady service revenue stream from our investment—so long as the prototype worked as designed.

You can probably guess what's coming. The day finally arrived when the product was unveiled, with great fanfare and publicity, at the Toledo, Ohio, headquarters of one of our customers. Everything went great...until several days later when we started to see electricity production results. The data showed the rooftop turbine performed worse than had the special funnel not been attached at all! The prototype blade was actually interfering with the pull-through of the wind.

It was an expensive unit and, without the benefit of superior wind generation, you couldn't justify—even with the tax credits—a return on investment. So that was that. It was one of my worst investment decisions ever, but in a way I'm glad I went through the experience. I learned a valuable lesson: that I am still very capable of making stupid mistakes and I should never shut down someone who's raising objections.

In fact, to this day I have a framed copy of the startup's stock certificate sitting on my desk to remind me to listen. Even if the people raising concerns turn out to be wrong, it is better to explore their objections than to ignore them and be blindsided later on.

It is also worth reminding readers that although the wind startup was a terrible investment, I didn't bet the farm. We bet $700,000, but we made over ten times that amount in net profit the same year. Nonetheless, if I had listened to my partner's objections, I could have avoided the loss. In hindsight, I would have structured the deal differently to be more performance based. But, because I was so determined to secure sole sourcing, I was blind to any objections. I wanted it too badly, and I got took.

When the race is on, and it's your time to pounce, **there is always going to be an element of risk involved.** It comes with the territory. Embrace the risk, but don't bet the farm!

RECESSION READINESS ASSESSMENT QUESTION #13

Do you have an excellent company culture, hire only awesome people, and immediately exit people who are not awesome or who don't fit your culture?

If you score yourself GREEN on this question, it means you hold quarterly meetings with all employees to update them on the current state of the company as well as the long-term strategic plan for the future. You also use these meetings to recognize those employees whose hard work, dedication, and loyalty have made a difference in the success of the company. You do this because you know employees who are recognized in this way have more job satisfaction and are more likely to stay with the company long-term.

If you score yourself green here, it also means you have an executive coach for yourself and your leadership team. This person works with you on business strategy and key issues, but also on your "life plan," a tool you use to reach your personal definition of happiness and success. Like the recession plan, the life plan is written in advance, before you really need it, when life is calm and you're in a rational state of mind—not when you're on the precipice of a major life decision. **Having a life plan and a coach for yourself and your leadership team—to promote individual growth—goes a long way toward establishing a strong company culture.**

A lot of companies pay lip service to culture, but don't reach beyond their comfort zone. Companies that are part of a franchise system, in particular, tend to over-rely on the other franchisees within the system—when what they should also be doing is networking with their competitors. If this sounds like you, score yourself YELLOW here. You may have the beginnings of a strong company culture, but if you're only talking to your own people, you're getting a monolithic perspective. Start networking with other companies who are doing things differently, so you can analyze their successes and failures—even if that means being brave and sharing your own stories first! Engage with peers and competitors at conferences and events, and pay special attention to what high-performing leaders at these conferences do during the breaks. (The real value of conferences is usually in the networking done in the hallways between speakers and workshops—and at the bar!)

You can't create culture out of thin air. You have to have the right mindset. If you scored yourself RED on this question, most likely your company is grinding it out and burning through people. It won't be easy to change. But if you're serious about starting to do culture *right*, you have to have a heart-to-heart with yourself and your leadership team about the legacy you want to leave. If you're ready to do that, to make the change, go ahead and follow the recommendations for yellow. Check out www.recession.com for more resources.

CULTURE, RECRUITING, AND RETENTION

Being ready for a recession means creating a strong culture, recruiting **the right people**—and having systems to retain them.

Nothing is more important than having the right people on your team. After all, they're the ones who are most in contact with your clients and vendors. They're like the tires on a car: they're where the rubber meets the road.

Fun fact: did you know that NASCAR tires don't have any tread on them? They're completely smooth. They're designed that way to get more surface-area contact with the track, which gives better traction. The tires actually become so hot that they melt slightly and get a little sticky, which creates even more traction.

This is a good way to think about building your team: you want your people to be "sticky" in their dealings with clients and vendors by instilling a service-driven relationship culture. If you don't have the right people, you can't build a strong culture—and you certainly can't 10X your business in a recession.

> Like NASCAR tires, the stickier you and your team are with your clients, the more traction you'll experience.

So how do you make sure you have a strong culture that will survive a recession? Start with your core values. As Gino Wickman wrote in his book *Traction*, the first step in building core values is to name the three to six people in your organization who you wish you could *clone*—meaning these employees are so great that, if you had replicas of them, you could dominate your market and industry and grow your business 10X. **Which of your best people would *you* choose to clone?** What are the characteristics that led you to put them on your list? This list of characteristics contains your core values.

The more creative your core values are, the better. You want prospective employees and prospective customers to "stub their toe" on your core values by not making them too self-evident. Values like "teamwork" and "integrity" are so overused that nobody pays attention to them. Values like "Lagniappe" (look it up!) or "Lunch

Second" will catch people's attention and let you tell your company's story.

CREATIVE CORE VALUE	OVERUSED CORE VALUE
Lagniappe	Honor
Spongy	Integrity
Flockable	Teamwork
Gluey	Fun
Fly the Airplane	Respect
Lunch Second	Quality
Everything-In-Between	Excellence
27.2™	Passion
Truth Tellers	Collaboration
Can Do Attitude	Innovation
Full Throttle	Accountability

Next, think about who you'd most **love to hire,** including people who currently have jobs or are otherwise unavailable. In Jack Daly's book *Hyper Sales Growth*, he writes: "The only way you can be effective at recruiting top people is to identify and go after them." He recommends having a target list of ten to fifteen names and focusing on the kind of people who are *not* looking for a job and are happy in their current position.

Daly recommends getting in touch with those ten to fifteen people twice a month, either over a meal or by email or phone. It may seem like overkill, but it's not. Again, life happens, and you never know when those A-players are going to suddenly be ready for a change (e.g., when their current employer changes their compensation structure without warning!). Daly writes: "The odds are that if you are courting them twice a month, life is going to happen in the next year to one or two of those 10 to 15 people." If you want more A-players, you'll need to increase the volume of candidates that you and your leadership team are courting.

This continuous process is how you need to think about hiring and recruiting. It's like a faucet left permanently running. Too many companies try to turn on the spigot when they need to make a hire and then turn it off again.

A-players need to be *cultivated* in your candidate pipeline.

CULTIVATING A-PLAYERS

Your company needs to be made up of 50 percent or more A-players. But this nirvana can only be reached when you have been able to successfully identify who these people are and where their strengths lie and have placed them in the optimal position for success in your company. By paying attention to the unique skills each employee brings, you are able to capitalize on their strengths.

In order to create highly effective teams, be aware of each employee's behavioral profile. It's critical that you put the right people together, teams that can work effectively without personality conflicts. The DiSC™ profile and Culture Index™ are valuable tools for placing everyone properly and empowering employees to interact with one another.

Be willing to move people around to find the optimal combination for each team. In the book *The Boys in the Boat* by Daniel James Brown, the author recounts the 1936 Olympic US rowing team and how coach Al Ulbrickson swapped boys in and out of the racing shells until he found a boat that achieved "swing" or that elusive quality of great teams that some describe as flow. A team that swings seems to glide over the water. You want the teams at your company to swing! Don't settle.

If you're like many companies, however, you have *some* A-players at the top of the organization or sprinkled throughout—but you aren't cultivating them at all levels. At Roth, Paul led a quarterly book club where he would have lunch and get all the high-potential

A-players together to review and discuss a business book like *What the CEO Wants You to Know* by Ram Charan. Doing something like this will break down silos, help establish friendships between departments, and nourish high performers.

Of course, it's unlikely that C-players (poor performers) will suddenly become A-players (top performers). You still have to focus on hiring the right people. Hire only people who meet your high standards; succumbing to pressure to fill a role with a second-rate candidate will only make things worse. This issue is exacerbated when the economy is strong and unemployment is low because hiring becomes even more competitive during those times.

> If your company is lacking in A-players, stay strong in hiring only people who meet your high standards.

If you allow yourself to hire below your company's standards, it will become a habit—and before long you'll have a company full of C- and D-players rather than A-players. To make matters worse, A-players prefer to work with other A-players. If you surround them with inferior talent, they'll wonder what's wrong with you as a leader and they'll leave.

Employee performance *must* be evaluated regularly. If

someone is not achieving their job responsibilities, you have two choices: train or terminate. **Don't continue accepting inferior talent.** At the highest levels of your company, if you are in growth mode, you will most likely have to recruit your way out of the problem versus training and developing existing talent. Your best option will depend on your internal pipeline of talent.

In any case, you need to constantly be hunting for A-players (and farming them from within your staff). You don't usually find A-players on an internet job board. They don't stay unemployed long nor do they "apply" for jobs in traditional ways. They almost always rely on their network to find their next opportunity. So, join their networks.

After cultivating your list of A-players and joining their networks, the next step is to brainstorm **behavioral interview questions** that you can ask potential employees to determine if they share your core values. For example, if one of your company's core values is going "full throttle," a good question might be "Can you tell me about a time in school, your last job, or your personal life where you went 'full throttle'? What did that look like?" If the candidate can't rattle off three to four full-throttle experiences off the top of their head, do you think they share that core value?

This interview question exercise will help you gain clarity around recruiting the right people, as part of being ready for a recession. Then you will need to think about *retaining* them. How do you keep great people happy so they don't quit?

Words are ephemeral: they fade into thin air as soon as you say them. Actions speak louder than words. Are the people in your company consistently displaying behaviors in alignment with your company values? Can you think of a way to use a symbol to bring your core values to life? For example, one company hands out little Gumby dolls to new employees to remind them of the value of flexibility.

Strong leaders spend time making sure they show their employees how much they value them. They write them thank-you notes, call them on their birthdays, and catch them in the act of living out a core value. What are some of the ways you can celebrate your employees? For inspiration, read *Make Big Happen* by Mark Moses.

JONATHAN: FREEING THE C-PLAYERS

I remember one time working with a company at a full-day strategic planning session, and there was a C-player who had been on their management team for a long time. After our second meeting, the leadership team and I decided that this guy wasn't happy. He hadn't been happy for a long time. At that very meeting, he agreed to leave the team. It was a mutual decision. We took a break, he packed up his bag, shook everybody's hand, and left the company on the spot.

That moment stuck with me because I think we realized all at once that, with this individual in his management role, we were never going to be able to keep growing the company. From that point on, we made sure the management team was all A-players, people who really bought into the vision and could execute against it. Looking back, it wasn't even a close call, and in my experience, once you have concerns about a leadership team member it almost never gets better. The only thing you usually get to decide at that point is when the separation occurs (sooner is better for all involved, by the way!).

Paul and I have seen many leaders agonize over letting someone who obviously is not an A-player go. Excuses we've heard include, but are not limited to: He/she has been with the company from the beginning. He/she is a family friend, he/she is my brother/sister, he/she doesn't always behave like a jerk...We've heard it all! Once the leader finally terminates the sub-par player from the company, then we hear: I should have done this months/years ago, I feel so much better, why didn't you tell me to do this sooner?

Think about it like you're the coach of an NFL team. Do

the Patriots accept C-players? The 2016 and 2017 Browns did. Do you want to win Super Bowl championships like the Patriots or go 1–31 like the Browns did over two recent, consecutive seasons? Committing to win is committing to surround yourself with A-players who live your culture of excellence.

Look around your company. The players (your people) who take the field at your company every Monday through Friday, do they look like the Patriots or the Browns?

Make sure you do an intense review—on a quarterly basis—of your talent in search of the best players to put out on the field. You need to be aiming to have the talent to win gold at the Olympics of your industry. Most companies don't. In fact, when we bring this metaphor up with leaders, they often admit that they don't even have the talent to *qualify* for the Olympics.

Don't accept C-players who are average contributors. Focus intensely on acquiring, cultivating, and developing talent. This characteristic is what sets the top-tier companies apart from the rest. **Top companies are willing to upgrade their people.** They follow a systematic process where people are evaluated fairly and objectively. When people are falling short of expectations, they have the necessary, honest, difficult conversations. (Read *Difficult Conversations* by Douglas Stone, Bruce Patton, and Sheila

Heen if you need more guidance on how to have tough talks with your team members.) Top companies put in place performance improvement plans and give people a chance—if the employees don't make a change, they're freed to pursue other opportunities.

With Fitness Together, I hired a lot of family members and it became complicated. There was a deep sense of loyalty (it was one of our core values!) and for the most part it worked out fine. But when you have C-players, especially if they're family, you *have* to let them go. If you don't, you'll send the message there's a double standard—and that can really start to erode the culture and impact the performance of others.

At the very least, you need to have a system in place for reviewing employees on a quarterly basis. How can you possibly get your C-players up to a minimum acceptable standard (or free them to go to a company where they would be a better fit) if you don't even have a system for evaluating them?

You need to start by accepting the fact that A-players don't like to hang out with B- and C-players. They quickly get frustrated and then they leave. If you are going to be mission-driven, then letting C-players stay will eat away at that mission and ultimately erode the culture.

> Have an employee review process in place that you follow on a quarterly basis to recognize your A-players and to free your C-players to move on to another company that is a better fit for them.

JONATHAN: WHAT DOGSLEDDING TAUGHT ME ABOUT TEAMBUILDING

Jonathan with Sled Dog Nanouk/Jonathan Slain

The dog I've got my arms around in the picture is named Nanouk. When I was on this dogsled in Canada with my Entrepreneurs' Organization Forum, I noticed Nanouk would run just fast enough to keep up, but not fast enough to have to pull any of the weight of the sled herself. All the other dogs were pulling against the towlines to take the weight of the sled and help move it forward. Nanouk? She was running just fast enough to keep up and not get dragged, without having to help shoulder the load.

Make sure none of your company's teams have a Nanouk.

A big part of recession planning is to **free the Nanouks.** The companies that do the best in a recession are the ones that take the time to regularly assess all their employees— and are willing to free the C-players so that they can go work for your competitors and not pull *their* sleds!

Over the years that I've been doing strategic planning with companies and working with their teams, I've come to believe that the most critical factor in being able to grow—and this applies especially during a recession—is a willingness to upgrade people. You can't afford to wait until you're *in* a recession to get the right team.

The companies that are willing to upgrade their people constantly are the winners.

When you're making above-average profit margins, it's hard to cut people that you've built a relationship with over many years. When a company is doing well, it's very hard to say, "Joe has to go," But it's vitally important for the future of your company that you do. **Don't let the fact that you're doing well cause you to be benevolent and soft.** Don't overlook the fact that someone is a C-player just because the work needs to get done and they can fog a mirror! Profit tends to mask people issues—

stay vigilant about assessing your talent and holding people accountable.

High-growth companies are very good at making effective and timely people decisions. They have honest, hard conversations with their people and give them three strikes. If they don't improve, they're out. Being able to make good people decisions is a key part of recession preparation. This means constantly trying to get more A-players and get rid of any C-players.

As Nickell, Rollins, and Hellman wrote in their article on recessions: "Sadly for some under-performing employees, the 'kick up the backside' [brought about by a recession] forced the firm to do what they should have done long ago—let them go."

Sometimes, say the authors, a kick up the backside is just what the doctor ordered: to force companies to change their ways and survive. Your choice is either to be the kicker or the kicked!

PAUL: HOW TO CONSISTENTLY EVALUATE YOUR CULTURE

I always ask leaders the following two questions: 1. Is more than half of your company made up of A-players? And 2. Do you regularly evaluate and free up your C-players?

My definition of an A-player is someone who you would want, or even need, to have on your team if you were starting your company from scratch. My definition of a B-player is someone who is important but not critical.

What about C-players? To me, a C-player is someone who you know you should probably fire, but you just haven't pulled the trigger for whatever reason.

I've seen many companies that didn't have the right players on the team—and that really puts a company at risk.

More to the point, if you don't have the right leaders on your management team—and you're not regularly firing the people who aren't right for top leadership roles—it puts you at an even higher risk in a recession.

RIGHTSIZING YOUR CAPACITY

If you are a company experiencing rapid growth, it is crucial you take the time to constantly re-evaluate your workload and rightsize your capacity accordingly. The only way to recognize gaps that need to be filled—talent and/or resource gaps—is to evaluate. As you do, you may find employees can be shifted to other areas of the company to better support your strategic priorities.

We recommend reviewing talent on a quarterly basis

to identify gaps in your most critical locations and divisions. Move your best people to your best opportunities; most companies reverse this best practice and task their brightest employees with cleaning up messes. Be careful you're not pigeonholing people into silos—and be flexible enough to move your talent to where they will make the biggest impact.

> Regularly move your best people to your biggest opportunities.

If you're like many companies, you *do* make these kinds of adjustments, but you do it reactively. It's not a proactive, systematic process. For example, you lose your largest customer and only then recognize that you have to downsize the company. Or, you win a big contract unexpectedly and only then realize you need to hire more people.

The problem with running your business this way is that when you rightsize on the fly, you run the risk of being overstaffed or understaffed. You are forced into the position of cutting jobs or scrambling to hire new employees and rush them through training. Sound familiar? Don't let yourself get into these situations. Have strategies in place to maximize the value of your business—and then use performance measurement tools to make the right people decisions in support of those strategies.

Remember: if you're not careful about making tough people decisions, you might wind up having them made *for you*—by your bank! We've seen this before and it's ugly! If you don't maintain your client base and you fool yourself into thinking you're going to get more new clients, you won't make the necessary adjustments. What may happen is that the workout group at the bank comes out to pay you a visit because you tripped your debt covenants.

> Rightsize your business continuously and make adjustments before your bank makes them for you!

PRACTICING FOR THE NEXT RECESSION

How severe is the next recession going to be? Which industries will it affect? Will it be like the last one?

Contractors, for example, got hammered in the Great Recession, and tech companies got crunched in the Dot-Com Recession of 2001.

> Learn from history. What lessons can you take from past recessions?

New information will always be coming at you, which is why it's so important to re-evaluate your plan for the next recession each quarter. Based on the new information, you might consider changing lanes or taking an off-ramp.

Should you be pivoting? Should you consider relocating? Should you be targeting an acquisition? These are the types of questions you'll answer at your quarterly recession practice sessions.

According to CJ Rhoads, "Executives should seek bargains and buy during a recession," taking advantage of the buyer's market and the lack of competition. For example, Banc One—based in Columbus, Ohio—used the 1990–1991 recession to aggressively acquire other banks and achieve their goal of becoming a national bank. They were able to pounce because they had practiced their game plan in advance and had the necessary conversations internally. These are conversations you need to be having, too, not just as a company but also *within each division.*

Don Greenland's recession strategy, as you'll remember, specifies that each regional *president* within the company works through the company plan individually and is empowered to trigger the tiered steps within their own groups. Important point: each leader is able to take action when needed. At Nabholz, they don't want to hold things up with red tape and "approvals." That's how you need to be thinking. **Each region, division, and department of a company should develop a mini recession plan,** as part of the whole. Each division should practice their part of the overall plan.

OTHER BEST PRACTICES

Recession planning is an ongoing journey, and we have a solid red light for you here. Avoid multiple rounds of lay-offs at all costs if it comes to that in a downturn. Cutting two people on Friday, and then two more the following Friday, and so on, is a terrible idea—it kills morale. **Cut once, cut deep** is our motto, and we got that from Daren Alexander, whose company, A-C Electric, does a great job of *practicing* downturn reduction with its leadership.

How exactly do they practice? According to Daren, the key is communication. In a lot of companies, the opposite is true. They think that every time they talk about something like a recession, it leaves a bad taste in people's mouths and stirs up negative emotions. As a result, they actually avoid talking about it. They don't bring it up on purpose. We believe the opposite is true. The more you talk about your recession plan, the better it is for people's psyches. Like Daren, we believe **it's impossible to overcommunicate.**

But that doesn't mean the communication should be off-the-cuff, disorganized, or haphazard. You need to be open and clear in your communication—and you need to have a *system* for doing strategic planning at your company, **a regular cadence of practice.**

Spend one day every quarter planning and building your

vision, and also use it to think about how you can keep eliminating waste from the business and improving your processes, including your recession plan. This is the essence of continuous improvement. What can you delegate, automate, or eliminate to reduce costs?

RECESSION READINESS ASSESSMENT QUESTION #14

Does your company have a continuous improvement process in place and do you regularly measure progress against established goals?

If you are GREEN in this area, you have a good process for recognizing and getting rid of waste—in labor, materials, and overhead expenses. Keep on doing what you're doing: focus on creating a company culture of continuous improvement. There are always ways to further streamline your systems and processes.

If you're like some companies out there today, you know about continuous improvement, and you're working to improve your processes and eliminate waste—however, you don't have an organized discipline around continuous improvement. If this sounds like you, score yourself YELLOW on question #14. You are well on your way, and you can start educating yourself more about continuous improvement. Read *2 Second Lean*[3] by Paul Akers and *The Goal* by Eliyahu Goldratt. Next, get the help of an expert to work directly with your team to implement continuous-improvement best practices.

If you haven't ever heard of continuous improvement (aka "Lean"), or have heard of it, but haven't started on your own journey, score yourself RED here and follow the instructions for yellow.

PAUL: THINK "BETTER, FASTER, CHEAPER"

As we discussed above, the key to staying in business over the long term is continuous improvement. Great! Now, how do you inspire your people to do it and own it?

When I was president of Roth, I implemented the Better, Faster, Cheaper (BFC) approach. I held employee meetings quarterly where, among many other items, I would explain how important it was to the survival of the business to continuously improve.

> How can you do your job **better**? How can you do your job **faster**? How can you do your job **cheaper**?

---

3   "Lean" is really just a fancy word for talking about continuous improvement and eliminating waste in a company.

Through the BFC process, employees asked themselves how they could do their jobs better, faster, and cheaper. Then they went through the exercise with their supervisors. In order to get the best results, I made sure that employees were empowered to speak up—that they understood that **no idea was too small to matter**. According to *Forbes*, American Airlines once did a BFC contest at the company and saved over $40,000 per year by removing one olive from each first-class meal tray. What olives exist at your company?

I also made sure supervisors embraced the program and encouraged this through measurement and posting of results. In your own companies, I recommend you measure the number of ideas generated per employee, averaging it per supervisor, and then posting those results. After that, do the same for the number of ideas *implemented*. Try to estimate the impact of these changes through metrics like money saved, time saved, or customer experience improved.

The more you can *show* the improvements, the more likely your people will be to continue to commit to BFC. Celebrating wins is also crucial. The *Rock the Recession Owner's Manual* lays the BFC process out in more detail.

WHAT IT REALLY MEANS TO EMBRACE CONTINUOUS IMPROVEMENT

A lot of companies *do* have a continuous improvement (Lean) initiative going, and they *are* regularly measuring progress against established goals. Sometimes, though, they make the mistake of getting sidetracked by whatever hot new business improvement idea people are buzzing about. This leadership ADHD is called the "Airport Bookstore Syndrome." Here's how it works: an executive will go on a work trip, stop at the airport bookstore, and spend the plane ride home reading the newest, latest, greatest business book. Then the executive comes back to the company and, even though they already have several initiatives going, decides to lob in a third new idea, or fourth, or fifth, based on the advice in the book they've just read.

The problem is that when you're constantly moving on to the next thing, you start to lose ground and backtrack on the progress you've already made. It's like having your foot on the gas *and* the brake at the same time.

According to a *Harvard Business Review* article about the Airport Bookstore Syndrome, "A particularly troublesome obstacle to sustained improvement...is initiative fatigue, which occurs when leaders jump too quickly from one improvement fad to another...Embarking on a new project is often more exciting than staying the course, but that doesn't necessarily deliver the best long-term results."

It's much better to pick a few priorities and really focus on those initiatives. As business guru John Milos says, "Put your eggs in one basket, and watch that basket closely." Then practice and refine. And then refine again. Or as Harvard Business School professor John P. Kotter puts it, "Never let up. Keep learning from experience. Don't declare victory too soon. When an organization takes its foot off the gas," that's when "cultural and political resistance arise." There's nothing wrong with creating *new* strategic initiatives once the old initiatives have had time to be successful and become part of the company's DNA.

Betsy Mack Nespeca, president of Mack Industries, has long believed in a culture of continuous improvement and people development. However, it can be tough to introduce a need for change through Lean concepts to a successful eighty-seven-year-old company. Although they made a strong leadership commitment to engaging their teams around continuous improvement, creating scorecards, and more, they initially encountered some resistance. They also found that being a multi-site company made it harder to implement with consistency.

Betsy makes a good point, and every organization will have its own unique challenges when it comes to implementing continuous improvement. The key is to stay flexible and continue to refine.

Refine, refine.

Implementing continuous improvement is an ongoing process. Not a single event. Unfortunately, that's how most companies treat Lean initiatives, and then they wonder why they don't work!

Practicing and refining drives improvement. Of course, practice and continuous improvement apply to recession planning as well.

*Please note that the aforementioned "Airport Bookstore Syndrome" does not apply to this book! Especially if you bought **Rock the Recession** in an airport or are reading it on a plane!*

RECESSION READINESS
ASSESSMENT QUESTION #15

Does your company's leadership team have an accurate method of tracking its backlog, its current work in progress, and its pipeline of potential new work?

At Roth, every business group had a pipeline they would present once a month in the company's executive team meeting. Any member of the executive team could call bulls**t on any other business group's pipeline—meaning they could challenge the probability of actually getting into contract and closing the deals in their pipeline.

Each business group would sort their projects into categories based on probability (i.e., the likelihood of actually closing each deal). Naturally, there was a huge amount of pipeline in the 25 percent or under category. No one paid much attention to this pile—it was more pipe *dream* than pipeline—but as the probability moved from 50 percent to 70 percent, the scrutiny started. At that threshold, Paul and his team were able to forecast with a fair degree of accuracy the amount of business they would close—which meant they could then adjust and recruit the talent needed.

If you're GREEN on this question, it means you're relentless about not only evaluating and measuring backlog but also calling BS on improbable deals like Paul and his team did at Roth. But if you're like a lot of companies, you're only halfway there: you *are* tracking your backlog—that's the easy part—but you're not tight on analyzing your pipeline. If this sounds like you, score yourself YELLOW on question #15.

Some companies have a bloated sales team because

their pipeline appears to require all of their sales people. But the truth is, much of that business is never going to close. What ends up happening is the company keeps all of their sales people around and then three or four years later—when they still haven't closed anything—finally lets them go.

A good way to avoid this pitfall is to give your sales staff a daily, weekly, monthly, quarterly, and yearly scorecard, which shows their number of closed deals and dollar volume of closed revenue. Very few people have the ability to actually ask for the order *and* close business. **Don't waste time—eliminate sales people who can't close.**

Moreover, when looking for sales professionals, we recommend that you use the DiSC™ profile or Culture Index™. These behavioral profiles help business owners and executives quickly ascertain how they can expect someone they hire to behave at work. Candidates can do the exercise online—it only takes about ten minutes—and company leaders will learn a lot from the results. Note that certain behavioral profiles are geared specifically to sales roles. And please consult your human resources professional or attorney regarding the use of profiles when hiring so as not to run afoul of the law.

If you're yellow on question #15, we recommend you engage a behavioral profiling expert to start hiring the right sales people and perhaps a fractional CFO to help evaluate your reporting (fractional CFOs are part-time professionals who work for several different companies simultaneously).

Now, if you don't review your backlog or pipeline *at all*, you probably already know you're in trouble. Are you in crisis mode all the time? Are you always in reactive rather than proactive mode, responding to facts and circumstances in the heat of the moment rather than being able to forecast and plan? Do you have way too much work, or conversely, no work?

If this sounds like you, score yourself RED on question #15, and start by hiring a behavioral profiling consultant and setting up a DiSC™ profile or Culture Index™ for yourself and your entire leadership team. You'll need to start deepening your self-awareness and really asking yourself the tough questions: Do you *want* to be in control of your business or are you content to continue to be reactionary? Are you ready to make a change? If so, follow the recommendations for yellow.

Does your company have a method to track the productivity of each employee?

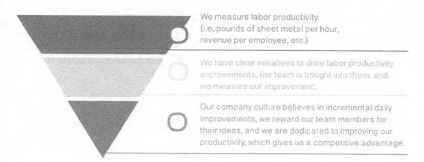

LABOR PRODUCTIVITY PYRAMID

We measure labor productivity.
(i.e, pounds of sheet metal per hour,
revenue per employee, etc.)

We have clear initiatives to drive labor productivity
improvements, the team is bought into them, and
we measure our improvement.

Our company culture believes in incremental daily
improvements, we reward our team members for
their ideas, and we are dedicated to improving our
productivity, which gives us a competitive advantage.

If you're GREEN on this question, it means your company has good labor productivity. Every employee knows his or her job, does it well, and works to improve performance regularly. Your people are well trained, and you have a system in place to encourage them to continue improving.

Keep doing what you're doing. Keep tracking productivity—and offering feedback so your people can maintain or better their production goals. It is essential that every person in the field or on the front line of your company knows what his or her production goals are for each day.

Some companies make the mistake of measuring productivity on a monthly basis instead of daily or weekly. If this is the case with you, score yourself YELLOW on question #16. Every company and team should have a huddle every morning and discuss expectations for the day, so the whole group knows what winning looks like. As humans, we want to win—and if we're not given a goal, we don't perform at our best. Make sure you're setting the bar as high as possible. Avoid the mistake of unknowingly encouraging mediocrity. If you're not measuring correctly, you're allowing people who are mediocre to hide in plain sight.

At some companies, the employees aren't given prescribed goals *at all,* at least not on an individual basis. If this is the case with you, score yourself RED on question #16. You need to adopt a new mindset and start paying attention to employee productivity. We recommend you read *The 4 Disciplines of Execution* by Chris McChesney, Sean Covey, and Jim Huling and *Measure What Matters* by John Doerr. Give your team daily goals to motivate them—and make sure to recognize them when they meet or exceed expectations.

RECESSION READINESS
ASSESSMENT QUESTION #17

Does your company's leadership team compare actual

financial results achieved against intended results at the completion of each project or quarter (whichever is most appropriate for your business)?

If you're GREEN on question #17, it means your company is vigilant about reviewing the status of projects and keeping track of progress. You look at your cash flow by project. You understand the importance of gross profit margins to the success of your business and give the necessary time and attention to conducting periodic job-cost reviews.

Fade is your profit slowly bleeding away into the atmosphere. It is the difference between your estimated gross profit and your actual gross profit. When your actual profit is lower than what you estimated, you're experiencing fade. It occurs anytime you expect to make a certain amount of money on a job or sale and you end up making less than what you expected. If you're not tracking fade, your business is leaking money. **Fade is your net worth running out the door!** You need to perform post-mortems on your jobs, projects, or monthly retail sales and figure out why you have fade. The only way to course-correct is to track this information.

As discussed in Daniel Coyle's book *The Culture Code*, the Navy SEALs are known for performing an After Action Review on every project. Your post-mortems should follow the same formula that the SEALs use. Ask yourself:

- What were your intended results?
- What were your actual results?
- What caused your results?
- What will you do the same next time?
- What will you do differently next time?

When Jonathan was at Fitness Together, he and his team measured their fade in terms of how many sessions of free personal training they had to give away when they made a mistake. Obviously, every time they gave away a session, it negatively affected their profit margin. Sometimes, Jonathan jumped to the conclusion that the giveaways were caused by poor employee performance. Often, the real problem was that they took on a lot of wrong clients to begin with. **Taking on a wrong job or project with a difficult client is almost always resigning yourself to fade from the start.**

In *The Pumpkin Plan* by Mike Michalowicz, the brilliant author talks about how if you want to grow a giant pumpkin, like they do at the state fair, you need to be constantly clipping all the small, runty pumpkins from the vine—because those runty ones steal nutrients from the giant pumpkin. Companies need to apply the same discipline as farmers: they need to be regularly freeing up problem clients that cause job fade by requiring a disproportionate amount of limited resources. Along the same lines, growth-oriented companies should be striving to work with ideal clients that have the potential to become giant pumpkins!

If you struggle with this issue, score yourself YELLOW on question #17. Your goal is to find the sweet spot where you *know* you're going to be able to deliver the job or service without cost overruns and without having to discount in order to get the project completed.

If you're not currently measuring your job fade *at all*, score yourself RED here. We recommend you meet with your CFO or controller, and possibly your external accounting firm, to design a job fade tracking process and report tailored to your business.

> We advocate you appoint a CFO—Chief Fade Officer. Their job is to discover the sources of fade and fix the root causes so that they don't repeat.

PRACTICE, PRACTICE, PRACTICE

By now you've done a great deal of heavy lifting in the first three gears of the Recession Gearbox Model. Your culture is tight, you're loaded with A-players, and you're tracking productivity and fade. But this doesn't mean you can slow down or coast. You must **always be practicing your plan.** Think of it as taking your recession plan out for a spin with your team. With these test drives, you'll see where adjustments are necessary to achieve peak performance.

Like 1st Gear (Assess), practicing is external to the economy. It's happening all the time. It's something you always need to do, regardless of what's going on in the outside world.

Practice means reviewing your plan regularly with your team. It means rehearsing for a recession so you're ready to pounce *at any time*. Remember, a recession isn't just a textbook economic downturn.

> A recession isn't just when the economy has two quarters of successive decline. Any major setback at your company or in your industry can lead to a downturn for you.

You may be thinking to yourself: *I'm ready. I've got this.* And that may be true; however, the point is you need to practice these initiatives *before* the punches start flying. As Mike Tyson famously remarked when he was asked about his upcoming fight with Evander Holyfield, "Everyone has a plan until they get punched in the mouth." Even companies that think they understand Mike's sage advice often don't practice enough and end up winging it with their team when something goes wrong. If you practice enough, you'll have the ability to take a blow and keep fighting. Don't let a recession punch you in the mouth!

In his book, *Make Big Happen*, CEO coach and entrepreneur Mark Moses tells a great story about being on a plane ride and encountering heavy turbulence. Instead of taking the opportunity to reassure the passengers, the pilot just pretended like nothing had happened. The problem is that when there is a lack of information, people tend to fill the void with their own—often irrational—assumptions. Moses compares this behavior to that of business leaders, who "often don't communicate clearly about what is happening and where things are headed—especially in uncertain times. Instead they lock themselves with their team behind closed doors to strategize."

Don't let that be you. Rehearse with your team before it's game time. Do you want your CFO and executive team to be looking at the news, freaking out, and backtracking? "I know we said we were going to buy this company, but now the sky is falling!" Or, do you want them to be executing against the solid plan you've been doggedly drilling?

If you get this right, you won't have to worry about backtracking. You'll have spent months, years even, getting your executive team together, working through the different scenarios: How would we handle layoffs? Who would send out the emails? You'll have worked through the list of who's getting laid off and who is going to send out the communications to the company and when. And you'll have practiced your strategic planning about target companies you're going to buy, who's going to contact them—and exactly how you're going to make the acquisition.

It's important to do all of this to become confident in the plan, to build up muscle memory like you do when you're learning to drive a stick shift, and also to *revise* the plan as needed. Every quarter your strategy must evolve, depending on what's going on within your organization—and in the economy.

TAKING ACTION

We reference many books throughout 3rd Gear. Select a book to read with your leadership team and start to improve on your biggest area of opportunity, whether it's related to improving your culture, increasing the number of A-players on your team, improving your productivity, reducing fade, or developing a regular routine of practicing your recession plan.

If you're not sure where to start, read the book *Traction* with your team and focus on the author's recommendations on how to establish a regular cadence of strategic planning meetings (where you can conveniently practice and continuously refine your recession plan).

CHAPTER FOUR

4TH GEAR—ACCELERATE

Instructions for using **The Recession Gearbox:**

⚙ 1st Gear (Assess) Always start with 1st Gear

⚙ Then engage 2nd Gear (Tune), 3rd Gear (Race), and/or 4th Gear (Accelerate) depending on "The Economy"

- If the Economy is in the Expansion or Recovery stages of the cycle, engage 2nd Gear, then 3rd Gear, then 4th Gear
- If the Economy is in Recovery or Contraction, engage 3rd Gear, then 4th Gear
- If the Economy is in Contraction or Recession, engage 4th Gear immediately if possible

🔧 Use the Emergency Brake at any point if needed

And, above all else, use your judgment to determine which Gear to use given the circumstances within your company and outside in The Economy

We have to be honest: this is our favorite gear. It's the most audacious gear because it's so against the grain. When most people think *recession planning*, they think,

"How do I survive? How do I just make it through to the other side?"

To us, that's not very sporting. What gets us pumped is thinking about how to grow—accelerate!—through the next recession.

PAUL: HOW I USED THE BLUE OCEAN STRATEGY

When my team at Roth and I were preparing for the recession, one of the less conventional things we did was read a book together. The book was called *Blue Ocean Strategy*, and the idea behind it is that, when it comes to strategic planning, it's better to swim *not* in the bloody red ocean of competition, but rather in the clean, calm blue ocean of innovation and differentiation.

You can see this in the way, for example, that Gary Burnison, CEO of the consulting company Korn/Ferry, transformed his organization by broadening its approach to the whole concept of recruiting. As he writes in the *Harvard Business Review*, "There's an analogy between an executive recruiting firm and a hospital emergency room. Clients come to recruiters only when there's a big problem, in the same way that people go to the ER only for emergencies...I wanted to diversify Korn/Ferry...to enable us to help clients with all their talent needs, so they wouldn't think of us only in moments of crisis."

In a red ocean, you're treading water in existing market space. You're trying to beat the competition and exploit existing demand. But **in a blue ocean, you're creating uncontested market space.** You're making the competition irrelevant by creating and capturing new demand like Gary Burnison did at Korn/Ferry.

Using the Blue Ocean methodology at Roth, we pivoted our company away from construction and toward service. We didn't *have* to make the change. We could have stayed how we were. We were doing okay in our 80 percent construction/20 percent service business, still making money. But we would have gotten killed in the recession, and would have had to do massive layoffs. Research shows that "companies that successfully adapt can emerge stronger than ever," while those that do not "face a Darwinist reality" (Journal of Business Research).

At Roth, I knew what was coming and saw the writing on the wall when it came to HVAC construction.

> I paddled like crazy with my team to get out of the red ocean before the recession wave crashed down on our heads!

PAUL: HOW I BEGAN WITH THE END IN MIND

I grasped the potential that lay ahead in HVAC and roofing services and energy management in a recession—so we decided that, instead of 80 percent construction, we were going to pivot to be 80 percent service. We **began with the end in mind** and looked ahead to what would happen in an exit situation. We knew that an acquirer would pay seven to eight times earnings for an annuity service business, but they would only pay book value, or at most two to three times earnings, for a one-off construction business.

In addition to moving from construction to service, we invested heavily in information technology. And we went green in a big way, focusing on sustainability and saving our customers on their energy usage and maintenance. We also branded ourselves accordingly. Together, these changes set us apart from our competition.

At the time, most companies accepted that their energy bill was what it was. We saw an untapped opportunity and were proactive about leveraging it. In a recession, companies are always looking for ways to reduce costs. We would tell prospective clients: "Here's what you'll get partnering with us. Here's the idea we have to help you reduce your energy expenditure. Here are the services we can implement on your behalf. Here's your expected reduction on your energy bill."

Our new approach was a huge success. We combined the

right strategy with the right team. We had great people and together we implemented the strategy well. We were heads-down and focused on results. This alignment is how we were able to **grow the company by double digits right through the recession**.

FILLING THE GAP

The Blue Ocean Strategy helps you understand what skills you're lacking. It helps you look critically at your business, see where you want to go—and what the gap is. But then you must have **a plan to fill that gap**.

For example, if you want to go from $25 million to $100 million in revenue, and want to enter different markets, but don't have the in-house talent to do it, then what you have is a "talent gap." One way to close that gap could be through acquisitions. Similarly, if you want to adopt continuous improvement practices within your company but don't have anyone on your team who is an expert—that would also be a talent gap.

Are you operating in Northeast Ohio and want to get into Pittsburgh but have no operations in Pennsylvania? That would be a geography gap.

The beauty of the Blue Ocean Strategy is that it gives you a springboard for filling these gaps. Of course, good ideas can come about anytime, with or without a formal strategy. However, when you use strategic planning with an eye toward thriving during the next downturn, it is especially powerful.

A recession can amplify the impact of strategic planning and **slingshot you past the competition**. There are so many opportunities; recessions are a wonderful time to stock up on cheap assets, people, and equipment.

JONATHAN: HOW I GOT MY EQUIPMENT ON THE CHEAP

As you'll remember from the Introduction, I got my ass kicked in the recession and had to borrow $250,000 from my mother-in-law to keep my fitness business from going under. However, there was one bright spot during those dark days: I had a really good relationship with the bank—CIT—that made SBA loans to many of the franchisees in the Fitness Together system.

One day, out of the blue, during the height of the Great Recession, the bank called to tell me that one of the other franchises was going out of business—and offered to sell me their equipment. The conversation went something like this: "Mr. Slain, there's a Fitness Together in New York that's going out of business. We own the loan and they've defaulted. We want to know if you'd be interested in bidding on their equipment."

Earlier, when I had bought this same equipment brand-new for one of my locations, I had paid over $50,000. But during the recession, it's not like I had a lot of extra money lying around. I knew I could scrape *some*thing together. So I told the bank I'd give them $2,000 for everything and come pick it up. I expected a quick "no" in response to my lowball offer. The bank got back to me an hour later and said, "Okay, let's do it. Can you send us the check now?"

It was a good day.

After picking up the equipment and driving it back to Cleveland, we sold the whole lot for $20,000, which helped us make payroll that week. That's how close to the edge we were.

Remember, I was still getting crushed by the recession. I didn't have a plan. But one thing I had in my favor was relationships—and in that scenario, I was able to leverage a strong relationship to get access to an opportunity I wouldn't have had otherwise. It was only because I had fostered the relationship that the bank thought to call me.

And even though I only paid the bank $2,000, it was good for them too. A win-win. When a bank writes off a loan, they're just looking to dump the assets attached to the deal. These are the kinds of opportunities you want to take advantage of during a recession. When banks are looking to dump assets that they've already written off—assets they just want to get off their books—that's when you can score some really good deals. **Everything is cheaper in a recession.** Talent is cheaper. So is the competitor you want to acquire. But in looking for bargain businesses to buy in a recession, you have to think about which sectors are likely to grow, not shrink, in a recession. Your acquisition will have a much better chance of success if it has a tailwind due to the recession. And you have to make sure your customer base is adequately diversified so you don't leave yourself overextended post-acquisition if some of your customers leave unexpectedly as a result of the downturn.

RECESSION READINESS
ASSESSMENT QUESTION #18

Is your company's customer base diversified?

Diversification of your business is the primary way to combat a recession, and if you're GREEN on question #18, it means you're well diversified. This was certainly the case for Paul at Roth. They had concentration in national retailers, but were also diversified with smaller accounts. Some of their retailers were recession prone while others actually did better in a recession (they were "countercyclical"). The important point is that none of their customers accounted for more than 10 percent of revenue. Plus, they were over $100 million in size, which by its nature meant they were well diversified.

If you are green on this question and have strong customer diversity, keep doing what you're doing and focus on end market and geographic diversity so you continue to lower your company's risk profile.

If you *lack* an intentional strategy to reduce your customer concentration and increase your diversification, score yourself YELLOW on question #18. Look into your business and see if you have any one customer that makes up a risky proportion of your business. Run through your customer list to understand how your portfolio will fare in a recession, and then be proactive in diversifying.

If you discover serious customer concentration in your business, change your score to RED. Unless you make a change and start reaching out to new customers, your business is going to be in serious jeopardy. Act to improve your situation so that no one customer represents more than 10 to 20 percent of your revenue.

RECESSION READINESS
ASSESSMENT QUESTION #19

⁓⁓⁓⁓⁓

Is your company's revenue diversified? Do you serve some market sectors that are countercyclical or unaffected by recessions?

It is also important to be diverse in terms of end markets and geographies if you hope to continue to grow your business. If you are strong on these items, score yourself GREEN on question #19.

It's not enough to be diversified geographically. If you're not also diversifying the products and services you're offering, score yourself a YELLOW here. You need to be diversified in *all* areas of your business. You need an intentional strategy to manage your markets, to recognize which markets are growing, which are stable, which are in decline—and then to act accordingly.

> Strong diversification in end markets lowers your risk profile.

Do a strategic review of who your main customers are and how they will behave in a recession. Have you ever looked at your top twenty customers and done a heat map (a graphical representation) of where they are geographically? It's essential that you understand what geographic markets you're in as a percentage of total revenue. If you have a large concentration of customers in the South, for example, and you know that area of the country is unlikely to grow or even remain stable in a recession, you need to consider how you can pivot before it's too late.

Act now. If you're in the RED on question #19, and have no strategy for end market or geographic diversification, your business is going to be seriously at risk until you analyze your market or geographic concentration and make the appropriate changes.

Read on for more tactical suggestions on how to find better end markets to serve in a recession.

WHAT END MARKETS/INDUSTRIES COULD YOU SERVE?

If we look back at the Great Recession of 2008–2009, we see certain industries got pummeled: manufacturing, finance and insurance, travel and tourism, and certain segments of the construction business. New car sales plummeted. Four-year university enrollment declined heavily. Casinos, hotels and motels, jewelry stores—all of these businesses took a big hit.

During The Great Recession

Industries that Grew or Held Steady	Industries that got Pummeled
Community Colleges	Certain segments of Construction
Grocery Stores	Jewelry Stores
Health Care and Social Assistance	New Car Sales
Guns and Ammo	Four Year Universities
Information	Travel and Tourism
Storage and Warehouse Leasing	Manufacturing
Veterinary Services	Finance and Insurance
Correctional Facilities	Casinos
Remediation /Environmental Cleanup Services	Hotels & Motels

Then there were other industries, like healthcare, that *grew* during the Great Recession, or at least held steady. Community college numbers went up. Grocery stores did well. Guns and ammunition, veterinary services, correctional facilities, multi-family housing, storage and warehouse leasing, remediation and environmental cleanup services—all of these were winners.

You can position your organization for growth in the next recession by researching end markets and industries that will grow or be stable in the future.

Where can you find this kind of information? It's not difficult. The secrets are out there, but they're not always free. In fact, here's a pro tip: purchase a subscription to the IBISWorld database, which will give you access to hundreds of different industry reports. Research firms, like IBISWorld, also put out newsletters with information about which industries are hot right now and which are forecasted to perform poorly. Seriously, it's like having the answer key to a test before you take it!

Industry	Revenue Growth % (2019-2020)
Solar Power in the US	28.4%
Wind Power in the US	27.5%
Hydraulic Fracturing Services	26.7%
Autonomous Underwater Vehicle Manufacturing	24.4%
Oil Drilling & Gas Extraction in the US	23.5%
Medical & Recreational Marijuana Growing	22.3%
Medical & Recreational Marijuana Stores	19.8%
Massage Franchises	18.0%
Natural Gas Liquid Processing	17.8%
3D Printer Manufacturing	17.5%
Peer-to-Peer Lending Platforms	15.9%
Social Networking Sites	14.5%
Automated Guided Vehicle Manufacturing	13.9%
Internet Publishing and Broadcasting in the US	13.8%
Field Service Management Software	13.5%
Online Children's Toy Sales	12.8%
Social Network Game Development	12.8%
Cyber Liability Insurance	12.2%
Ship Building in the US	12.1%
Solar Panel Installation	12.1%
Mining in the US	12.0%
Precision Agriculture Systems & Services	11.5%
Relaxation Drink Production	11.5%
Search Engines in the US	11.2%
Dark Fiber Network Operators	11.1%
Online Men's Clothing Sales	10.9%
Cementing Oil & Gas Well Services	10.9%
Online Apartment Rental Services	10.8%
Residential Senior Care Franchises	10.4%
Fraud Detection Software Developers	10.4%
Armored Vehicle Manufacturing	10.1%
Telehealth Services	9.9%
Internet Hosting Services	9.7%
Online Small Electrical Appliance Sales	9.6%
E-Commerce & Online Auctions in the US	9.6%
Wireless Internet Service Providers	9.3%
Fast Food Chicken Franchises	9.1%

Source: IBISworld.com

According to one recent IBISWorld report, all of the following industries are projected to grow: "tortilla production, wineries, vitamin and supplement manufacturing, software publishing, VoIP, IT consulting, video games, marijuana growing, and a host of online retailers." Some of these industries may be off the beaten path, but if there's an opportunity for you to start a relationship with a company in one of these fields, why wouldn't you?

If, for example, you sell your services to clients that are mostly in high-end retail (which will have tough times in a recession), you may diversify into selling your services (if appropriate) to tortilla factories, vet clinics, and hospitals—all of which will continue on or grow in a recession if history is any indicator of future performance.

Further, we see in the IBISWorld research that healthcare tends to be recession-proof, at least the "necessary" services provided by hospitals, ambulances, and diagnostic laboratories (in contrast to services like sports medicine and home healthcare). We learn that non-durable goods—such as food, fuel, cleaning supplies, paper products, and clothing—fare better than durable ones such as automobiles, furniture, consumer electronics, and appliances: "Durable goods were crushed during the Great Recession, while tubes of toothpaste and deodorant sticks still flew off the shelves."

Finally, there are opportunities to be had in countercyclical industries like insurance, food, home remodeling and maintenance, and alcoholic beverages. "During periods of recession," they write, "consumers must continue their expenditures on necessity products such as food and healthcare."

The answers are out there when you take the time to look. You need to read, and then you actually have **to put together a plan to leverage the opportunities that you discover.**

> If you want to get run over by the lucky bus in business, you've got to be standing in the middle of the street!

And if you learn that a particular industry dropped 17 percent in the last recession, and you happen to be overexposed to it in your own business, maybe take that as a warning sign—and start taking action to diversify and exit that industry!

It is very important to diversify your end markets and limit your exposure to any one industry. People make this mistake all the time. They think, for example, that because the last recession involved the housing bubble, they'll be fine as long as they're not vulnerable to the effects of a similar crash. But that's just not the case. **Not all recessions are built the same.**

> Diversify your revenue to make sure you have stability during recessions, as well as a platform for growth.

Either "you're growing or you're dying," says Betsy Mack Nespeca, president of precast concrete company Mack Industries. The growth may not happen immediately, but you have to be on a growth, or acceleration, path. During the last downturn, although Betsy's company actually shrunk in some of the existing markets it served, ultimately it grew as a whole, thanks to all the new areas of business it pursued.

"We had to be very agile and try new things," says Betsy. Prior to the recession, a majority of their business was in housing and subdivisions. They served several segments of these industries: highway, municipal, federal, commercial. All had been severely impacted by the residential decline and were now effectively dead. There was very little activity. So, in order to survive, they had to replace these parts of their business with something else. They focused on projects with *funding*. For example, they pursued several large projects for Veterans Affairs, which they knew was funded by the federal government. Ultimately, this strategy—among several others to leverage their diversity—allowed them to not only survive the recession but come back bigger and better.

HOW TO BE THE DISRUPTER, NOT THE DISRUPTED

Sometimes, diversification of end markets isn't enough to lead you to a blue ocean. When you're trying to think outside the box and do your Blue Ocean strategic planning, part of what you need to think about is how technology is going to disrupt your industry—what that will look like and how you can be part of it. Embracing new technology may be your life raft out of the red ocean.

There are signs everywhere. Again, you just have to look. Traveling in Tokyo, for example, Jonathan took the following picture of a ramen vending machine that is disrupting how everyone in Japan orders noodles!

Jonathan with Ramen Vending Machine in Tokyo/Jonathan Slain

Here's another example. How about the world's first self-driving pizza truck? As soon as you place the order, in fact, it starts driving to your house, and makes the pizza en route. It spits out the dough, puts the toppings on the pizza using a robotic arm, and delivers the finished pizza right to your door. Couldn't be any fresher if it came out of your own oven.

To be clear, we're not saying you have to be the first company with an idea like a self-driving pizza truck. You just have to be in on the innovation before the rest of your industry has shifted and you find your company doing something in an outdated, inefficient way. Blue Ocean Strategy doesn't mean you have to be completely alone where *nobody* else is swimming (although, if possible, this is a very lucrative place to be). It's just about going to a less crowded area of the ocean versus the bloody red surf where everyone is frantically fighting for the same small piece of business. To put it another way, you don't have to be creating the wave, but you want to be on the front edge of the wave—to get in on the leading part of the technology.

Jonathan (and His Wife Katherine) Diving with Sharks/Jonathan Slain

Most companies are swimming with the other sharks. They're jockeying for position in heavy traffic. You want to pull away from the rest of the pack. You don't want to be stuck with them.

In the construction industry, for example, people tend to be way behind the technology curve. As a group, contractors don't think they have to change the way they work quite yet. Everybody is still kind of waiting in limbo to see what happens. But in reality there are all sorts of exciting innovations happening in construction right now, from 3D printing to robots that lay bricks (aka SAM, the Semi-Automated Mason).

New technology is like toothpaste squeezed out of the

tube. It's just not going back in. Get in on it before it's too late.

Think about how you can **step on the gas** during a recession and create an action plan that you'll activate once the downturn is imminent. Learning to Rock the Recession™ isn't just about how you survive the next downturn. It's about the massive opportunities that a recession creates. It's about the potential to accelerate and achieve the kind of exponential growth you've always dreamed of.

PAUL: HOW I USED THE FOUR ACTIONS FRAMEWORK

In figuring out how to achieve this kind of exponential growth, my team at Roth used an excellent exercise from *Blue Ocean Strategy* to guide us. We applied something from the book called the Four Actions Framework to help us determine the best plan of attack.

The **Four Actions Framework** is also sometimes referred to as the ERRC Grid, which stands for Eliminate, Reduce, Raise, and Create. First, you ask which factors that your industry has long competed on should be *eliminated* from the business? Next, which factors should be *reduced* (well below the industry's current practice), and which should be *raised* (well above the industry's current practice)? Finally, what products or services should be *created* that your industry has never offered?

The point of all this planning work is to add new value to your business and guide your strategic planning.

The Four Actions Framework guides your strategic planning by forcing you and your team to confirm your current practices and identify new practices that add value.

When it comes down to it, the ERRC grid, and the Blue Ocean Strategy in general, are not that different from a classic SWOT analysis. Companies have long used this construct—of analyzing Strengths, Weaknesses, Opportunities, and Threats—as a means of determining their best strategic plan.

What I like about the Blue Ocean Strategy, and so does Jonathan, is that it's more actionable than SWOT. It's stuff you can do right away. You can apply your answers to your own business and begin eliminating, reducing, raising, and creating right away. The whole model is great because it gives your team license to throw ideas against the wall and see what sticks.

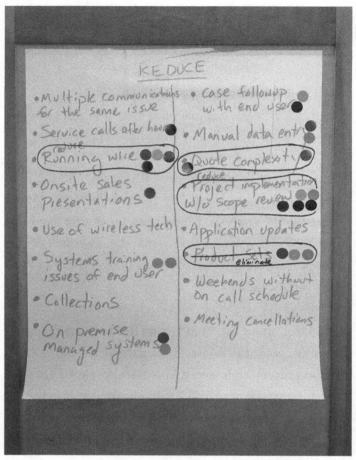

Blue Ocean Planning with Jonathan's Client—Integrated Precision Systems/Jonathan Slain

We have seen breakthroughs happen when companies do this Blue Ocean ERRC Grid exercise. For example, IPS (Integrated Precision Systems) is a leader in enterprise-level security systems. When they went through this process with Jonathan facilitating, their leadership team concluded that one thing it could massively *reduce* was running cable. The work of running cable is low-value and can be outsourced. Moreover, IPS's clients don't care who actually performs that commodity work (in fact, their clients probably prefer that IPS focus on the intellectual property of overall security-system design rather than pulling cable!)

Point is: by doing the ERRC exercise—and thinking about what they could Eliminate, Reduce, Raise, and Create—IPS became aware of a terrific opportunity to eliminate or massively reduce the time they spend running cable. Now, the company is taking steps to outsource the lower-margin parts of its work, so they can focus instead on opportunities for future growth, like moving more of their operations (and their clients' operations) to the cloud.

> What would you eliminate, reduce, raise, and create in your business?

TAKING ACTION

Having come to the end of this chapter, what we want you to do here is run through the *Blue Ocean Strategy* exercise of eliminate, reduce, raise, and create with your leadership team. Then, take it a step further and run through the exercise with a cross section of your entire company, including the field (or front line). In our experience, the employees closest to your customers often have the best ideas. And, after this exercise, you're going to ask your employees why they never shared their brilliant ideas on what to eliminate or create with you. And they're going to say: "Because you never asked!"

For more detailed instructions on conducting this Blue Ocean exercise, please email Jonathan@Recession.com and he'll send you a free copy of this section of the *Rock the Recession* companion workbook.

CHAPTER FIVE

THE EMERGENCY BRAKE

Instructions for using The Recession Gearbox:

- ⚙ 1st Gear (Assess) Always start with 1st Gear
- ⚙ Then engage 2nd Gear (Tune), 3rd Gear (Race), and/or 4th Gear (Accelerate) depending on "The Economy"
  - • If the Economy is in the Expansion or Recovery stages of the cycle, engage 2nd Gear, then 3rd Gear, then 4th Gear
  - • If the Economy is in Recovery or Contraction, engage 3rd Gear, then 4th Gear
  - • If the Economy is in Contraction or Recession, engage 4th Gear immediately if possible

⬛ **Use the Emergency Brake at any point if needed**

And, above all else, use your judgment to determine which Gear to use given the circumstances within your company and outside in The Economy

We're almost at the end of the book. Are you ready to Rock the Recession?

Not so fast. At this point, you are *almost* there: you've got a great strategy outlined that you can implement during any downturn. However, strategy requires skill in implementation. You will need to adapt as required based on the conditions of the road. What if your plan hits a pothole? What if you're in a recession and trying to race, but it's just not working? You may have to pull the **Emergency Brake** to save your business. If that happens, you want to do it without crashing.

Pulling the Emergency Brake in the Recession Gearbox Model is about cutting overhead as necessary to stay profitable or at least not lose money. As discussed in Chapter One, your recession plan will include an Emergency Brake section with different **tiers.** The idea is that if you reach these thresholds, they will be your trigger to pull your Emergency Brake, change your business model—and **reduce expenses.**

Again, tiers allow you to lay your plan out in advance and to do so analytically, so you don't go numb and make emotional, suboptimal decisions. You don't have to crawl through the crippling stages of grief like Jonathan did when his business fell apart during the recession.

JONATHAN: MY SEVEN STAGES OF GRIEF

For me, it was only natural to go through the well-documented emotional stages of grief during the Great Recession. When the recession was happening, these emotions clouded my judgment. There are seven stages of grief (a modified Kübler-Ross model) and when hard economic times hit—including job losses and salary reductions—I can attest to their validity:

#1	SHOCK	Initial paralysis at hearing bad news.
#2	DENIAL	Trying to avoid the inevitable.
#3	ANGER	Frustrated outpouring of bottled-up emotion.
#4	BARGAINING	Seeking in vain for a way out.
#5	DEPRESSION	Final realization of the inevitable.
#6	TESTING	Seeking realistic solutions.
#7	ACCEPTANCE	Finally finding a way forward.

The Stages of Grief Model

Again, going through these phases in a crisis is completely normal and even healthy. In my experience, it takes time and you don't get to skip any of the stages: in order to get to the final stages of testing and acceptance, you have to process all the information and emotions in the first five steps. Trust me, it is better to practice with your management team in advance, rather than during a downturn.

Another reason to complete this final leg of your recession planning: having tiers in place helps you act swiftly, which is incredibly important in a recession.

Imagine your business is losing a $100,000 a month and you're four months from running out of cash. If you don't act swiftly, if you waste two weeks freaking out, you'll be $50,000 closer to bankruptcy.

Social science experiments show that people make terrible decisions under stress. In addition, human beings have a "recency bias," meaning we give the most recent information we've heard more credibility than information we've had for a while, even if it's not more credible.

Recession tiers help protect you from your innate biases. Instead of making poor, emotional decisions because things are cratering around you—your cell phone won't stop ringing, you're getting angry emails from your banker and payroll company, frightened employees are standing at your door—you will be making smart, rational choices that have been thought out well in advance.

Human beings are imperfect. It's that simple. And that's why it's so important to have a tiered Emergency Brake plan. Still don't believe us? Consider the following: did you know that CEOs nearing retirement spend less during recessions than CEOs with longer career horizons? According to academic research, when a CEO has a long career still ahead of him or her, chances are the company is going to come out of a recession better because the CEO is willing to make tough but necessary investments.

Think about that for a moment. We assume CEOs are going to make optimal decisions, or at least decisions they believe are best for their organization. As it turns out, however, this one random factor—of how close the CEO is to retiring—has a major impact on their behavior and their recession spending.

Do you really want your career, and your company's future, to be based on something as trivial as how close the CEO is to retirement? Of course not, and that's why it's even more important to come up with a rational plan, as a team, in the cool, rational light of day—so you can minimize the effect of the disruption that accompanies every recession.

Does your company's leadership team have a way to measure for early warning signs that your business is headed in the wrong direction?

If your company has a plan with agreed upon metrics to warn you of an approaching recession in your business, then give yourself a GREEN on question #20. For example, if you have written out and agreed that if your revenue ever drops by 20 percent (20 percent is just an example), you'll make specific cuts to overhead (and you've outlined those cuts in writing), you are green.

If you kind of have a plan, but it isn't fully written out, then score yourself a YELLOW. Your next step is to keep reading this book and the *Rock the Recession Owner's Manual* and get your plan down on paper and further spelled out.

Finally, if you're driving along with the top down, completely exposed, with no way to know if or when it's going to start thunder-storming, score yourself RED. Pull over! Start by having your team meet to discuss the issues presented in the upcoming pages related to how to set your recession-plan tiers. Use the *Rock the Recession* companion workbook to guide your progress.

SURVIVAL: PROTECT THE GOLDEN GOOSE

When you're in the situation where the recession is here and you can't grow through it, where the only option is to pull the Emergency Brake, you're simply not going to survive without a lot of pain unless you already have a written plan with the tiers in place. **You've got to protect the Golden Goose at all costs** (the business is the Golden Goose and/or **you** are the Golden Goose).

This is true whether the recession is external or internal. For example, we have one client that is a $5 to $6 million company and has been around for a long time, a third-generation, family-owned business. They didn't have a recession plan, didn't establish tiers, and then the unthinkable happened: they lost their top customer, Walmart. This is a perfect example of an internal recession. It had nothing to do with the broader economy. It was simply a matter of Walmart deciding to consolidate their vendor base—and unfortunately for our client, they weren't one of the chosen few.

Overnight, they found themselves in a recession, since Walmart was such a large customer for them. They lost over 20 percent of their volume, and in the following years, they lost close to $1 million. Ever since, they've been trying to get back to where they started, but are still struggling. Imagine the pressure: your business has been in the family for generations, and now you're going to be the one who potentially loses the company that your grandparents founded.

Sounds terrible, right? Contrast that with the example of Don Greenland's company, which we talked about in Chapter One. As you'll remember, he and his leadership team, at the request of the company's board of directors, developed their own recession plan before the Great Recession. Although their tiers and triggers were slightly different than what we recommend, they were very well-thought-out. Some of the steps are triggered on a corporate-wide basis, while others are triggered by division or by executive committee. Most impressive, he and his company continue to update their tiered plan on a regular basis. They updated it before the last recession, in the midst of the recession, and postrecession. To this day, they are regularly revising the plan.

Or consider John, the billboard king who Jonathan met on the plane. Again, although John doesn't have a formal tiered recession plan in the way we recommend, he inherently understands the Emergency-Brake concept. He pays close attention to his billing, and looks for ups and downs. Having been in the business for forty years, and having been through three recessions, he knows what has to be done proactively if he starts to see certain patterns in his billings. He doesn't wait until it's too late. He sits down regularly with his sales people and looks at the numbers—how many inquiries and renewals they are receiving—and he is ready to pump the brakes as necessary to avoid a crash.

In short, before the Great Recession, Paul had a plan. Billboard John had a plan. So did Don Greenland's team. All had their Emergency-Brake tiers and knew what they had to do if they ever hit those numbers.

Jonathan's fitness business, Sebastian's landscaping business, and the company that lost Walmart as a customer did not have an Emergency Brake planned, and they hit the wall.

> Fear and uncertainty can cripple you and your business in a downturn and cost you a lot of money; that's why you need a plan for when you are going to pull the Emergency Brake.

Know your Emergency-Brake numbers. Have your tiers in place. Make sure everything is predetermined and can happen almost automatically.

Your plan also needs to take into account the fact that not all recessions are built the same way or have the same depth—and that's where the different tiers become truly valuable.

Some recessions might just take you to Tier One or Tier Two (overhead expense reductions), while others are going to immediately zoom you to Tier Three or Tier Four (massive layoffs and pay cuts). Some are going to give you mild opportunities to pounce, whereas with others—especially if you have cash, don't have debt, and are in good financial shape—you can go hog wild snapping up assets!

HOW TO SET YOUR TIERS

In the following pages, we explain exactly what needs to happen in Tier One, Two, Three, and Four. First, you need to figure out how you're even going to know trouble is approaching. It's different for each organization, which is why you need your own custom Dashboard, complete with warning lights, to indicate a recession ahead.

Why are the warning lights on your Dashboard different from other organizations'? Every company has their own version of the so-called canary in the coal mine. If you're not familiar with this expression, it comes from the days when miners literally took a canary down into a mine. They knew that if the bird fell off its perch, it meant there was too much carbon monoxide, and they better get out of there.

How does this apply to recessions? Take, for example, our friend Mike Lancaster, who was actually the one who first used the canary line in this context. He is an owner of the Frank L. Blum Construction Company. That's his "mine," and in the work that he does he talks to a lot of architects. When those architects signal their pipeline of work is slowing down, Mike knows that trouble is probably looming. The architects are his canaries.

Who or what are your canaries? What are the metrics in your business most likely to change your behavior? Of course, there are many potential answers here: revenue, profit, backlog, or pipeline, for example. But for the purpose of your Dashboard, less is more. What are the two to three most critical metrics? And what are your blind spots? What are the key metrics in your business that warn you of trouble ahead—or that prevent you from backing up over a cliff?

To give you an example, a key metric for one company we work with is their number of marketing inquiries. Before the Great Recession, they saw a big drop-off in the number of marketing inquiries they were getting online, and then the recession hit. So for them, they're paying close attention to that number.

To figure out what your best indicator is, talk to your team. Talk to your accountant, your lawyer, and your banker. Your answers will spell out what you need on your Dashboard and for your tiers.

TIER ONE

At Tier One, your Dashboard is indicating trouble ahead.

This means it's time for you to eliminate all the dead weight that's accumulated, the unnecessary overhead in your business. Time to stop making those discretionary donations. Time to cancel your industry journal subscriptions (or let them expire). Reduce vehicle allowances. Limit entertainment expenses. Suspend any country-club memberships tied to your business. Forget about those exotic locations for company-planning retreats. Double up on offices, or sublease half of your offices.

As CJ Rhoads puts it, now is the time to "attack your budget with a scalpel and not a machete."

Remember: these decisions may not be permanent. You're just postponing any discretionary capital expenses. So instead of replacing your air conditioner, for example, you're having it serviced. You're getting rid of things like third-party janitorial or lawn maintenance. Instead, you're going to take out your own trash and cut your own grass. Oh, the horror!

Why do you have to do these things? It's simple: in this example, you've dropped from 100 percent of your normal revenue to 80 percent, which was the threshold for activating your Tier One Emergency Brake plan and starting to make these cuts and doing away with all the "nice-to-have" expenditures in your business.

Most important, because you've set your tiers in advance—worked it all out with your team proactively and achieved the necessary buy-in—there's no confusion or hesitation. Everybody knows that if revenue or income drops to the specified level, the cuts are going to automatically kick in.

To be totally honest, these Tier One cuts are likely the kinds of changes you should be making anyway, even when your company is thriving and firing on all cylinders. It's just good business hygiene, and we would wager that, no matter how well you're doing, you could trim some fat. *Especially* when you're doing very well.

> Do you really need the first-class plane tickets and the elite country-club membership and the fifty-yard-line tickets for football games?

Certainly if you've reached the Tier One threshold—and your Dashboard's check engine light is on—that's your cue. You know the time has come and you know what you have to do, because you have a firm plan in place.

Unfortunately, what we usually see is that when a company's revenue drops—whether the economy is in recession or not—the company's leaders are slow to respond because they haven't prepared. Maybe the owner doesn't want to cut their country-club membership, so they put it off until next month—and then another month goes by, and another. Next thing they know, they're busy golfing while their company can't make payroll!

Having a plan protects you from yourself.

And if someone really doesn't want to lose their country-club membership, maybe that will inspire him or her to work that much harder in the meantime so the company doesn't have to do Tier One cuts!

TIER TWO

At Tier Two, your Dashboard is flashing, which means that **unless you start to brake, you're going to crash.** This is where you get into a deeper round of expense cuts. If you're at this stage, you need to be suspending all discretionary expenses, as well as any industry conferences you were planning to attend. In fact, by now you should be reviewing all expenses, regardless of whether or not you budgeted for them.

One interesting and counterintuitive aspect of Tier Two cuts is that even though you should indeed be eliminating advertising expenses related to branding, **you should actually be increasing (or at least maintaining) your**

marketing for clients. This is a very common mistake companies make: they start cutting all their marketing expenses because it's what their gut tells them to do. Strange as it may seem, research shows your marketing dollars actually go further in a recession. During an economic downturn, most people are cutting back on their marketing, so it becomes much easier to afford things that maybe you couldn't before, like TV advertising. Additionally, with fewer people doing marketing, you can take market share from your competitors.

A study by economists Gary L. Lilien and Raji Srinivasan shows how the companies that did best during the 2001 recession in the United States were the ones that saw the downturn as an opportunity and implemented a marketing response to capitalize on the opportunity. The authors term this behavior "marketing productivity." According to them, "Firms with the will (the nerve or culture), the skill (marketing and customer knowledge and the ability to turn that knowledge into strategy), and the till (resources to fund investments in a downturn) are amply rewarded both during and after the recession."

> Take advantage of the fact that marketing dollars go further in a recession.

We know, for example, that casinos got hit really hard in the last recession. Sandeep Khera was working in the marketing group at Caesar's at the time. Caesar's is one of the largest companies in gambling and entertainment. Sandeep confirmed to us that the industry got its butt kicked. But he also said that he and his team used this time to retrench and actually grow their business by focusing more on segmenting their clients and tailoring their marketing messages.

We hear the same thing from Christie Hefner, former CEO of Playboy Enterprises. During her tenure at the helm of the organization, she was one of the longest-running female CEOs of a public company on record. And she did an amazing job: not only did she and her company play offense when going into recessions, but they also spent more—not less—on marketing during these downturns.

Point is, she understood the value in—and the opportunities presented by—a recession. While other people were dropping out of advertising and marketing, she was thinking differently. Bigger. She paid attention to what was going on in the economy and acted strategically on that information. For example, she knew that when gas prices were high, it affected newsstand purchases. People went out less, drove around less, and bought fewer magazines from the stands. Knowing newsstand sales would drop in a recession, she knew she had to compensate with increased marketing.

To reiterate: cutting down on expenses in Tier Two is indeed important, but you're not just cutting to cut. It's all about making smart cuts. It's about cutting with a return-on-investment mindset. Think about the cyclists on the Tour de France. The strongest competitors don't attack on the flat or early in the race, but rather on the roughest, deepest, most grueling sections. They attack on the uphill stages or the cold, rainy stages when their competitors are feeling low and ready to quit. It's the same with recessions. When times are toughest, that's when you want to attack with marketing.

During the Great Depression, for example, Procter and Gamble heavily promoted some of its best-known brands, including Camay, Ivory, and Crisco. In the 1990–1991 recession, GM did the same with its Saturn Division. Similarly, during that time, Intel Corporation launched its "Intel Inside" promotion, taking advantage of the fact that there was little advertising competition. De Beers did the same with their "Shadows" program. Finally, in the Great Recession of 2008–2009, we saw companies like BMW investing heavily in marketing.

Beyond marketing, studies show that R&D investments made during recessions increase both profit and stock returns. According to data analyzed by Sanjiv S. Dugal and Graham K. Morbey, "These results—consistent across two recessionary periods—show that sales declines are far less likely to occur in companies that invest significantly in R&D."

Moral of the story: be like the cyclists and attack when everybody else is out of energy or conserving their energy for a finish that they might never get to see.

> Don't just cut expenses to cut. Make smart, strategic cuts.

Other Tier Two cuts include freezing hiring for all open positions and postponing any building maintenance. You will also want to embrace creative initiatives like job sharing, where two full-time employees share one full-time employee position rather than a situation where one person stays and one person has to be laid off. Another idea is to reduce temps and support staff to match your new workload.

TIER THREE

Tier Three means that your Dashboard is blaring at you and you must take further action to avoid disaster. **Tier Three is where the tough "people decisions" have to be made.** Our philosophy here, when it comes to laying people off, is to "cut deep and cut once." Do it all in one fell swoop, not in dribs and drabs. Have a list of everybody in your company, all your employees, how long they've been with you, their total compensation (including their salary and all their benefits)—and then rate them as As, Bs, or Cs. Change your grading system from "I like him/her" to "Do I think they have the talent to perform?"

The classification system goes something like this: A-players are critical. They're the ones who you would absolutely need if you were starting your business again from scratch. B-players are important, but not critical. C-players are gone at Tier Three. But remember what we told you in the chapter about 3rd Gear. Do you recall Nanouk, the dog that ran just fast enough to keep up but not actually pull the dogsled? If you have C-players, Nanouks, on your team who you know need to go, but you just haven't been able to find the courage to cut them loose, **the recession is a great opportunity to deal with the people and the issues that you've been avoiding**.

Tier Three of your Emergency Brake plan is not fun, but there's no way around that. What matters is that you deal with it in advance, not in the moment. Not when you're emotional. Imagine a worst-case scenario: you've got an employee who's been with you for a really long time. He just came into your office and explained to you that one of his kids is really sick. That's a tough conversation to have at any time. But now imagine you've already prede-termined that this employee is not one of your strongest people, and that he has to be let go at Tier Three. It's still going to be hard to fire him, but at least you'll have already gone through the phases of grief about it. You'll be ready, and you won't back away from what needs to be done to protect the Golden Goose and the livelihoods of all of your remaining employees.

Tier Three is the time to be laying off part-time employees. Furthermore, we encourage you to consider accelerating employee retirements. You are doing anything and everything you can to avoid the pain of getting to Tier Four because, while Tier Three is very difficult, Tier Four will make you up and cry.

Now for Tier Four, which hopefully you will never get to...

TIER FOUR

Tier Four means your Dashboard is flashing non-stop, indicating that your company's very existence is threatened. In fact, your company is now in a depression of its own, regardless of what the economy is doing. **The only way you are going to be able to continue this race is to make an immediate Pit Stop and overhaul your engine!**

In Tier Four, all remaining staff—A and B employees—take pay cuts. You simply can't afford to pay everybody what you're paying now. The leadership team takes a 20 percent pay cut. Senior management takes a 15 percent cut, and everybody else 10 percent. You will set your own percentages; we're just getting you started with these numbers. As leaders you must lead; cut your salary first— and take the most significant cut. When Jonathan gave a *Rock the Recession* keynote address at a meeting of steel fabricators, one owner shared that in the last recession, he took a 100 percent pay cut and his eleven employees all took 50 percent salary reductions. (They survived and their business is stronger than ever; each of the eleven employees now owns stock in the company.)

Again, it's not pretty, and we hope you never have to live through Tier Four. However, you still have to plan for it, so your people can have the important conversations with their spouses about the possibility of having to take a major pay cut.

It makes all the difference when you take a responsible approach like this. When you have a tiered system, you and your team talk it all through, often years in advance. You practice it regularly. Your people are part of the decision-making and the execution. This is what achieves buy-in, protects morale, and ultimately creates resilience.

> We believe—strongly—the pain of writing out Tier Four means you will fight hard to never have to implement Tier Four.

That's the people side of the equation in Tier Four; in addition, all process improvements or cost reductions will also be on the table at this point. You will be **selling assets and eliminating less profitable divisions**. Having a tiered plan allows you to decide in advance what you would sell and in what order. Instead of waiting until your back is against the wall and you have to liquidate, you can do it in a way that still allows you to protect the Golden Goose. You'll live to fight another day because following every recession is a recovery.

TAKING ACTION

Having come to the end of this chapter, what we want you to do here is—regardless of where you are in the process—**consider making your Tier One recession plan cuts now** even if you don't need to.

Why do we want you to do this now? For one thing, these are the easiest cuts to make. But the real reason is **every business has excess expenses**, especially in boom times. Every business needs to periodically review their expenses and trim the fat.

Moreover, activating Tier One is a good way of starting to *practice* what it will look like when you go all-in on your recession plan.

Do it now. Get rid of 10 percent of your overhead, and then put that 10 percent in the bank for the next recession. As you have learned, a recession is inevitable. It may come sooner, or it may come later. No matter when it comes, our question to you is: isn't it smarter to get rid of some overhead and save that money in cash now—so you can *pounce*?

Our *Rock the Recession Owner's Manual* workbook has detailed, step-by-step exercises to help you and your team develop your Emergency Brake plan.

NOW GO AND POUNCE!

JONATHAN: OH, HOW THINGS CHANGE

On July 20, 2018, I remember going to my local bank branch. It was a beautiful day in Chagrin Falls, Ohio. The birds were singing, the sky was blue, and every stoplight turned green right as I approached it.

That was the day I went to the bank and picked up a cashier's check for $58,849, the exact amount I still owed my mother-in-law. I flew down to her home in Myrtle Beach, South Carolina, and proudly presented her with the final payment of my debt in person. **That was the moment when I understood how important it would be to help others avoid the pain that I endured by not having a recession plan.**

Paul and I wrote this book because we want you to be prepared before the next downturn arrives.

WHERE TO GO FROM HERE

Remember, the Recession Gearbox Model you have explored in this book is **not linear, it's cyclical**. You're going to engage different gears depending on where we are in the economic cycle: recession, expansion, recovery, and contraction.

Whatever happens, you'll have a leg up on the competition because, unlike them, you're not complacent. As you've discovered through these chapters, **what gets people destroyed during a recession is *complacency*.** Leaders who think the good times are going to keep on rolling forever. They're out there driving around aimlessly with no plan for achieving breakout profit during the next recession.

You know better. Whatever happens now in the economy, or within your own organization, you'll be prepared for it. You'll know what to do since you have a plan. You may have felt shaky when you first set out on this recession-planning journey—now, like learning to drive a stick shift, it has become natural and instinctive. It's just a part of how you do business.

You've practiced, you've refined—and now recession planning is something that is always going to be there with you, always going on in the background, as you tend to all the other important parts of your business, like marketing, sales, strategy, operations, and finance.

Knowledge is power. It is our hope that you will now feel *empowered* to leverage the next recession and actually look forward to the opportunities.

As for us, we can't wait.

Now, go out and **Rock the Recession**!

APPENDIX A

RECOMMENDED READING LIST

Recommended Reading

The Black Swan
by Nassim Nicholas Taleb

The Entrepreneur's Guide to Running a Business
by CJ Rhoads

Traction
by Gino Wickman

Blue Ocean Strategy
by W. Chan Kim and Renee Mauborgne

The Pumpkin Plan
by Mike Michalowicz

Recommended Reading

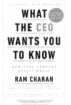

What the CEO Wants You To Know
by Ram Charan

Hyper Sales Growth
by Jack Daly

Make Big Happen
by Mark Moses

Difficult Conversations:
How to Discuss What Matters Most
by Douglas Stone, Bruce Patton and Sheila Heen

2 Second Lean:
How to Grow People and Build a Fun Lean
Culture at Work & at Home
by Paul A. Akers

Recommended Reading

The Goal
by Eliyahu Goldratt

The 4 Disciplines of Execution
by Chris McChesney, Jim Huling, and Sean Covey

Measure What Matters
by John Doerr

The Culture Code
by Daniel Coyle

PAUL'S AND JONATHAN'S RECESSION READINESS ASSESSMENTS

Recession Readiness Assessment™

Complete online at www.Recession.com/ready

Name _____Paul Belair_____   Date _____2008_____

Company _____Roth Bros_____   Position _____Owner + President_____

Our goal is to ensure you are in the best position to capture the opportunities a recession brings. One of the first steps in our journey together is for you to benchmark your company's "recession readiness."

Readiness is defined as the state of being fully prepared. Our Recession Readiness Assessment will give you a quantified answer for just how prepared you are for the next downturn. This assessment is a systematic analysis of your company's ability to perform, removing guesswork and emotion, which will allow you to identify strengths and potential challenges for your company in the next downturn.

Once you have this information, you will be ready to hit the road armed with the knowledge of where you want to go and guidance from us on how to get there.

. . . .

INSTRUCTIONS:

Please take approximately 10 minutes of uninterrupted time to complete the assessment. Answer the 20 items using the following scale:

GREEN: YES/ALWAYS

YELLOW: MAYBE/SOMETIMES

RED: NO/NEVER

WHITE: Wave this flag if you don't understand the question or if you honestly have no idea how to answer. We encourage you to use this option if it applies, as waving the white flag will result in the best possible recommendations for you and your company.

Once complete, you will receive an email with your results and score.

. . . .

Recession Readiness Assessment

Complete online at www.Recession.com/ready

1st GEAR ASSESS

	YES/ ALWAYS	MAYBE/ SOME	NO/ NEVER	I DON'T KNOW

1. Does your company have a written action plan for the next recession or major shock to your company's system (i.e., losing your biggest customer)?

2. Does your company's leadership team understand and track basic economic indicators (for example, the yield curve and the unemployment rate)?

3. Are your company's vision, mission, and values documented in writing and exemplified daily through behaviors at all levels of the company?

4. Does your company have a written, long-term, focused strategic plan and do you spend at least one day each quarter updating it?

2nd GEAR TUNE

5. Does your company's leadership team understand the financial health of its major customers and vendors?

6. Is your company's EBITDA (Earnings Before Interest, Taxes, Depreciation, and Amortization) margin "best in class" for your industry?

7. Does your company have five to ten percent of its next twelve months of estimated revenue as equity on your balance sheet?

8. Does your company's leadership team regularly meet with its bank representatives to discuss the company's line of credit to ensure the limit is right for current and future business needs?

9. Does your company's leadership team know all restrictions in place on any company debt and do they review these "covenants" monthly to ensure compliance?

10. Do your company's owners regularly review any personal guarantees on company debt and are they actively working to reduce them to zero?

Recession Readiness Assessment

Complete online at www.Recession.com/ready

	YES/ ALWAYS	MAYBE/ SOME	NO/ NEVER	I DON'T KNOW
11. Does your company have cash or debt available to fund growth?	✓			
12. Does your company have a board of advisors that meets at least quarterly with the leadership team to help set plans for growth, ask challenging questions, and hold the team accountable for its action plans?	✓			

 3rd GEAR RACE

	YES/ ALWAYS	MAYBE/ SOME	NO/ NEVER	I DON'T KNOW
13. Do you have an excellent company culture, hire only awesome people, and immediately exit people who are not awesome or who don't fit your culture?		✓		
14. Does your company have a continuous improvement process in place and do you regularly measure progress against established goals?	✓			
15. Does your company's leadership team have an accurate method of tracking its backlog, its current work in progress, and its pipeline of potential new work?	✓			
16. Does your company have a method to track the productivity of each employee?	✓			
17. Does your company's leadership team compare actual financial results achieved against intended results at the completion of each project or quarter (whichever is most appropriate for your business)?	✓			

 4th GEAR ACCELERATE

	YES/ ALWAYS	MAYBE/ SOME	NO/ NEVER	I DON'T KNOW
18. Is your company's customer base diversified?	✓			
19. Is your company's revenue diversified? Do you serve some market sectors that are counter-cyclical or unaffected by recessions?	✓			

 EMERGENCY BRAKE

	YES/ ALWAYS	MAYBE/ SOME	NO/ NEVER	I DON'T KNOW
20. Does your company's leadership team have a way to measure for early warning signs that your business is headed in the wrong direction?	✓			

Recession Readiness Assessment

Complete online at www.Recession.com/ready

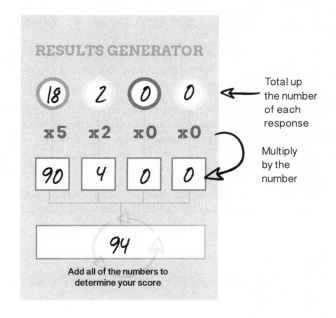

RESULTS GENERATOR

18	2	0	0
x5	x2	x0	x0
90	4	0	0

Total up the number of each response

Multiply by the number

94

Add all of the numbers to determine your score

Higher is better!

85 - 100 = LOOKING FORWARD to the next Recession!

60 - 84 = Need to START PREPARING for the next Recession!

0 - 59 = High risk of FAILURE in the next Recession!

Recession Readiness Assessment™

Complete online at www.Recession.com/ready

Name **Jonathan Slain** Date **2008**

Company **Fitness Together** Position **Owner**

Our goal is to ensure you are in the best position to capture the opportunities a recession brings. One of the first steps in our journey together is for you to benchmark your company's "recession readiness."

Readiness is defined as the state of being fully prepared. Our Recession Readiness Assessment will give you a quantified answer for just how prepared you are for the next downturn. This assessment is a systematic analysis of your company's ability to perform, removing guesswork and emotion, which will allow you to identify strengths and potential challenges for your company in the next downturn.

Once you have this information, you will be ready to hit the road armed with the knowledge of where you want to go and guidance from us on how to get there.

· ·

INSTRUCTIONS:

Please take approximately 10 minutes of uninterrupted time to complete the assessment. Answer the 20 items using the following scale:

🚩 **GREEN:** YES/ALWAYS

🚩 **YELLOW:** MAYBE/SOMETIMES

🚩 **RED:** NO/NEVER

🏳 **WHITE:** Wave this flag if you don't understand the question or if you honestly have no idea how to answer. We encourage you to use this option if it applies, as waving the white flag will result in the best possible recommendations for you and your company.

Once complete, you will receive an email with your results and score.

· ·

Recession Readiness Assessment

Complete online at www.Recession.com/ready

 1st GEAR ASSESS

	YES/ ALWAYS	MAYBE/ SOME	NO/ NEVER	I DON'T KNOW

1. Does your company have a written action plan for the next recession or major shock to your company's system (i.e., losing your biggest customer)?

2. Does your company's leadership team understand and track basic economic indicators (for example, the yield curve and the unemployment rate)?

3. Are your company's vision, mission, and values documented in writing and exemplified daily through behaviors at all levels of the company?

4. Does your company have a written, long-term, focused strategic plan and do you spend at least one day each quarter updating it?

 2nd GEAR TUNE

5. Does your company's leadership team understand the financial health of its major customers and vendors?

6. Is your company's EBITDA (Earnings Before Interest, Taxes, Depreciation, and Amortization) margin "best in class" for your industry?

7. Does your company have five to ten percent of its next twelve months of estimated revenue as equity on your balance sheet?

8. Does your company's leadership team regularly meet with its bank representatives to discuss the company's line of credit to ensure the limit is right for current and future business needs?

9. Does your company's leadership team know all restrictions in place on any company debt and do they review these "covenants" monthly to ensure compliance?

10. Do your company's owners regularly review any personal guarantees on company debt and are they actively working to reduce them to zero?

Recession Readiness Assessment

Complete online at www.Recession.com/ready

	YES/ ALWAYS	MAYBE/ SOME	NO/ NEVER	I DON'T KNOW

11. Does your company have cash or debt available to fund growth?

12. Does your company have a board of advisors that meets at least quarterly with the leadership team to help set plans for growth, ask challenging questions, and hold the team accountable for its action plans?

 3rd GEAR RACE

13. Do you have an excellent company culture, hire only awesome people, and immediately exit people who are not awesome or who don't fit your culture?

14. Does your company have a continuous improvement process in place and do you regularly measure progress against established goals?

15. Does your company's leadership team have an accurate method of tracking its backlog, its current work in progress, and its pipeline of potential new work?

16. Does your company have a method to track the productivity of each employee?

17. Does your company's leadership team compare actual financial results achieved against intended results at the completion of each project or quarter (whichever is most appropriate for your business)?

 4th GEAR ACCELERATE

18. Is your company's customer base diversified?

19. Is your company's revenue diversified? Do you serve some market sectors that are counter-cyclical or unaffected by recessions?

 EMERGENCY BRAKE

20. Does your company's leadership team have a way to measure for early warning signs that your business is headed in the wrong direction?

Recession Readiness Assessment

Complete online at www.Recession.com/ready

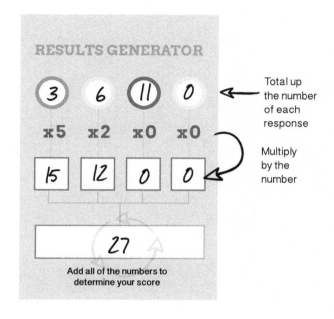

RESULTS GENERATOR

(3) 6 (11) 0

← Total up the number of each response

x5   x2   x0   x0

15   12   0   0

← Multiply by the number

27

Add all of the numbers to determine your score

Higher is better!

85 - 100 = **LOOKING FORWARD** to the next Recession!

60 - 84 = Need to **START PREPARING** for the next Recession!

0 - 59 = High risk of **FAILURE** in the next Recession!

APPENDIX C

PAUL'S TOP TEN LIST FOR ACHIEVING YOUR DREAM OUTCOME IN LIFE

1. Develop a life plan that projects out fifty years into the future (update your spiritual, family, financial, career, physical, mental, friends, social, and give-back goals quarterly).
2. There are only so many Saturday nights—don't waste time with people who do not have your back when you truly need it, who do not bring you joy, or who gossip.
3. Always have goals to learn and grow. Thank those who have helped you to learn and grow.
4. Help others succeed as often as possible.

5. Do random acts of kindness as often as possible.
6. Take care of the Golden Goose (you and your business are the Golden Goose).
7. Engage slowly (employees, friends, and significant others) and let go quickly when it's not going to work.
8. Stay humble regardless of how many commas are in your investment/bank accounts. Your IQ doesn't increase because you have money. Thank everyone who has helped you along your journey.
9. Do not take yourself too seriously, EVER!
10. Still figuring it out!

ABOUT THE AUTHORS

JONATHAN SLAIN, AUTOBAHN CONSULTANTS

Jonathan is the "governor" of Recession.com and principal of Autobahn Consultants. His purpose is to help others realize their Dream Outcomes by helping business owners and their teams get results, make tough decisions, improve team health, and develop the right strategies.

Jonathan is the expert on recessions and the Entrepreneurial Operating System™ you want guiding your team. He coaches high-growth leadership teams around the world to implement EOS™, also known as Traction. As an EOS Implementer™, he focuses on helping leaders get what they want from their businesses. Jonathan spends one-hundred-plus days a year implementing Traction with teams just like yours.

Jonathan focuses on companies that are looking to double their top and/or bottom line within the next three to five years.

Jonathan owned and operated fitness franchises for ten years, holding the place of honor as the top unit of more than five hundred. It was his time there that gave him the real-world, hard-knock-life experience that allows him to claim his title as an expert on recessions.

Jonathan spent two years in investment banking. He worked on mergers and acquisitions totaling over $500 million in enterprise value.

PAUL BELAIR, 10X CEO COACHING, LLC

Paul is the "accelerator" with Recession.com and founder of 10X CEO Coaching, LLC. His passion is helping leaders grow their companies, create good jobs, and build wealth.

He ran and owned Roth Bros., Inc., a national specialty contractor, for fifteen years and cut his teeth coming up through the financial ranks as a CPA/MBA.

During the Great Recession, under Paul's leadership, Roth's revenue grew to $150 million. By putting the right strategies in place, fostering the right culture, and building a high-performing, results-oriented organization, Paul and his team were able to achieve this rapid growth.

Then, sixty-three months after investing in the purchase of Roth, Paul led the sale of Roth to a large global company. That sale resulted in a once-in-a-lifetime creation of wealth for both Paul and his team with a return that was over seventy times the amount of their initial investment. They turned a $1 million investment into over $70 million in a little over five years.

Paul is the chair of the Construction Industry Network for the Young Presidents' Organization (YPO), serving 2,300 contractors worldwide. He is a member of Peter Diamandis's Abundance 360 group and an investor in early-stage tech startups like Vingapp.com, BuiltWorlds, and Bold Capital.

ACKNOWLEDGMENTS

JONATHAN'S ACKNOWLEDGMENTS:

First and foremost, a very special thank you goes to my mother-in-law, Anne Newcomb. She took a gigantic chance on me when she let me marry her favorite daughter. Then she took another big chance when she loaned me the money to keep my business going in the last recession. Along the way, she never said a word about the money, unless it was to check in with me to make sure I was doing okay. Everyone needs a mother-in-law like Anne in their corner. Thank you! And, don't worry, I'm NEVER borrowing money from you again. (Well, let's say, probably not ever again, but "never" is so final...I mean, what if there's a great opportunity?)

I want to thank Dr. Katherine Slain, my wife; she puts the "rock" in *Rock the Recession* because she is always there to support my crazy ideas and keep me grounded. I'm so proud of her and so lucky she said "yes" over a decade ago. Next, I want to thank my daughters: Caroline and Anne Penney. They are my Slainiacs! They share my time, sometimes begrudgingly, with all of my clients and audiences, and I know that even though they are only six and eight years old, they support me because they know how happy this work makes me.

I have to thank my admin (and older sister), Wendy, "The Brakes," for providing so much lagniappe (look it up!). I also want to thank Jay Berkeley for his loyalty and support on all of my projects. Indeed, I write this on a plane ride home from the MCAA Convention where Jay was the reason the show went on! I also have to thank my sister Allyson; she was my "other mother" growing up and shaped much of who I am today. Mom and Dad, thank you for all of your love and support. You've helped raise our girls while Katherine and I have been pursuing our career goals. If they turn out like Wendy, Allyson, and me, then the world better watch out. You did good!

And I must thank my brother-in-law Michael. Without Michael, I wouldn't have had the adventures with Fitness Together that led to this book. Thanks for rescuing me from the fluorescent landscape of investment banking. I also want to thank Brad Newcomb for his contribution to this project; without him, I wouldn't be married to

Katherine. He also taught me how to really drive stick, contributing to that metaphor being included in the book.

I have to thank my Entrepreneurs' Organization forum mates: Lynlee Altman, Joe Coughlin, George Hohman, Lisa Lewis, John Neubert, Gunner Puhl, and Matt Radicelli, for listening to me drone on and on about this project and providing insight at our meetings. There is no better forum in EO than Outperforum!

Beyond my forum, EO has given me an incredible list of mentors. My current mentor, Jerry Grisko, and past mentors John Milos, Mike Neundorfer, and Don Taylor, all generously donated their time to meet with me and shape my future. I want them to see that the effort has paid dividends. I continue to strive to make them all proud!

During my pursuit of this first book, there were a couple people who were in the right place at the right time for me, providing important guidance, and I'm not even sure they know how influential they were, so I want to thank: Mike Michalowicz (author of *Clockwork* and several other books), Michael and Amy Port (the founders of Heroic Public Speaking who helped me launch my speaking career), Brian and Staci Inskeep, and everyone that contributed an interview to this book for taking the time to support Paul and me. And a few special mentions to those of you who took a chance on me and referred me to your entire networks when I was first getting started with my consulting career: Jade Chang Sheppard and Aaron Grossman.

Thanks to my *Rock the Recession* team: Yasmin Swartz (the best designer on the planet), Jason Cook and Frank Wasinski (IT and marketing gurus), and Darla Klein (adult learning expert, brilliant refiner of the recession model, and the most thoughtful editor of this manuscript, you made this book shine). Each of them has an amazing ability to take a half-baked idea and sculpt it into a beautiful finished product. They are the very best of what they each do, and as much as it pains me, I am printing their names here so the world can discover and hire them for their projects. But, I swear, you all better not drop me when you get even more clients added to your already very busy calendars. We still have a lot of work to do together on future projects!

And I have to thank our entire team at Scribe Media, especially our tireless scribe, Mark Chait. Mark—I tortured you with rewrites throughout this process to get the book perfect. You hung in there with me and the final product is proof. Heaven help you for having to listen to hours of tape of me and Paul!

Don't worry Mina, I didn't forget you! To my Doberman, Mina, thank you for spending countless hours lying on the couch while watching me work, and for coming over and putting your head in my lap when I needed to take a break.

Finally, I want to thank all of my Traction® clients and *Rock the Recession* keynote audiences. When the next downturn hits, I expect each and every one of you to *Rock the Recession*!

PAUL'S ACKNOWLEDGMENTS:

I want to thank the following mentors who guided me throughout my life:

Formative Years—Mike Coudriet (Hoban High School teacher and freshman basketball coach) saved my high school experience and changed my trajectory; Dan Kramer and his father, Steve (high school basketball coach and summer-job boss)—they both believed in me and taught me the power of Positive Mental Attitude (PMA); Vince Kopy (University of Akron accounting teacher and mentor to me and to many accounting students)—he showed me the way to escape from my circumstances.

Work Career—Rick Crouse (partner at PWC), the hardest working, smartest, and most humble leader I ever worked for—pushed the hell out of me, Ken Waldron (Gentek Building)—Ken believed in me and taught me if you can't get it done in forty hours, either you are not effectively working or your direct reports are not effective, Kitty Dindo (Roadway/Caliber and First Energy)—believed in me and gave me tremendous opportunities to grow and learn from her, Sam A. Roth (humble leader and visionary who gave me the opportunity of a lifetime to run Roth), Kevin McHugh for helping to change my team's mindset from employees to owners and for being a go-to rock for me, my YPO Forum Mates for always being there for me and encouraging and pushing me, Barry Schlouch for encouraging me to step up and be a leader in the YPO Construction Industry Network, Matt Gray for letting me help, in a very small way, get BuiltWorlds going, and Mark Moses for showing me how a coaching business works.

I also want to thank Kelly Blazina for being a pain in my ass, but for helping me evolve to the person I am and for always having my back; Paul Miller for being the perfect example of a wonderful dad, husband, and friend; and Chris Johnson for the privilege of allowing me to get to know him and work with his team.

A special thanks goes out to my family for putting up with me and for making life so special!

BIBLIOGRAPHY

INTRODUCTION

William Thornton, "Did the recession make Alabama more obese?" in *AL.com*, October 23, 2018.

Donald A. Redelmeier and Robert J. Tibshirani, "Are Those Other Drivers Really Going Faster?" in *Chance*, Vol. 13. No. 3, 2000.

CHAPTER ONE

Xiaorui Huang, "Ecologically unequal exchange, recessions, and climate change: A longitudinal study" in *Elsevier's Social Science Research*, March 6, 2018.

Ranjay Gulati, Nitin Nohria, and Franz Wohlgezogen, "Roaring Out of Recession" in *Harvard Business Review*, March 2010.

Zachary A. Powell, "Burnin' Down the House: The 2007 Recession and the Effect on Arson" in *Deviant Behavior*, 2017.

Kate Julian, "The Sex Recession" in *The Atlantic*, December 2018.

Harold M. Zullow, "Pessimistic rumination in popular songs and newsmagazines predict economic recession via decreased consumer optimism and spending" in the *Journal of Economic Psychology*, September 1991.

John Mauldin, "Economic Brake Lights" in *Thoughts from the Frontline*, November 2, 2018.

John A. Pearce II and Steven C. Michael, "Strategies to prevent economic recessions from causing business failure" in *Elsevier's Science Direct*, 2005.

CHAPTER TWO

David Nickell, Minna Rollins, and Karl Hellman, "How to not only survive but thrive during recession: a multi-wave, discovery-oriented study" in *Journal of Business & Industrial Marketing*, 2013.

CHAPTER THREE

David Nickell, Minna Rollins, and Karl Hellman, "How to not only survive but thrive during recession: a multi-wave, discovery-oriented study" in *Journal of Business & Industrial Marketing*, 2013.

Matthias Holweg, Bradley Staats, and David M. Upton, "Making Process Improvements Stick" in *Harvard Business Review*, November–December 2018.

John P. Kotter, "Accelerate!" in *Harvard Business Review*, November 2012.

CHAPTER FOUR

Gary Burnison, "Korn/Ferry's CEO on Transforming the Company in Mid-Crisis" in *Harvard Business Review*, December 2013.

Rick Buczynski and Kenneth I. Brown, "Flying Blind into the Next Recession? (Part 2)" in *IBISWorld*, February 2, 2018.

John A. Pearce II and Steven C. Michael, "Strategies to prevent economic recessions from causing business failure" in *Elsevier's Science Direct*, 2005.

CHAPTER FIVE

Dilek Gulistan Yunlu and Dianne D. Murphy, "R&D Intensity and Economic Recession: Investigating the Moderating Role of CEO Characteristics" in *Journal of Leadership & Organizational Studies*, 2012.

Raji Srinivasan, Arvind Rangaswamy, and Gary L. Lilien, "Turning adversity into advantage: Does proactive marketing during a recession pay off?" in *Elsevier's International Journal of Research in Marketing*, 2005.

Gary L. Lilien and Raji Srinivasan, "Marketing spending strategy in recessions" in *Australasian Marketing Journal*, Vol. 18, pages 181–182, 2010.

Sanjiv S. Dugal and Graham K. Morbey, "Revisiting corporate R&D spending during a recession" in *Research Technology Management*, July–August 1995.

If you're ready to
Rock the Recession,
your next step is to purchase the *Rock the Recession Owners Manual*

www.recession.com/shop

Step-by-step instructions to develop a written recession plan for your company.

Recession.com

ROCK THE RECESSION:
OWNERS
MANUAL

INDEX

Akers, Paul, 2 *Second Lean,* 143, 215

AL.com, 15, 239

Alexander, Daren, 140-141

Altman, Lynlee, 235

American Airlines, 144

American Dream Exit, 19, 20, 113

anger (grief stage), 188

annuity businesses, 41, 87, 163

"Are Those Other Drivers Really Going Faster?" (Redelmeier and Tibshirani), 239

arson for profit, 55-56

Assess

    emotions in, 41

    as first step, 27-28

    leadership teams and, 69-70

    predicting recessions in, 58-61

    preparation and, 43-46, 55-58

    in Recession Gearbox Model, 28

    recession plans and, 46-51, 64-65

    in Recession Readiness Assessment, 31

    winning and, 40-43

asset base, 65

asset sales, 95, 207

The Atlantic, 56, 239

Australasian Marketing Journal, 241

Autobahn Consultants, 229

B

B-players, 137, 204, 205-206

balance sheets, 87-91

Banc One, 140

banks and bankers, 75, 90-93, 95-96, 98-101, 139-140, 165-167

bargaining (grief stage), 188

behavior, 66-69, 130, 196

behavioral interview questions, 129-130

behavioral profiles, 127, 149-150

Belair, Paul, *43*

    advice of, 89, 227-228

    background of, 62, 230-231

    as company president, 40-43, 52, 66, 86, 127-128, 143-144, 167, 180-181

    lessons learned by, 85, 116-120

    as mentor, 17-18, 23

    Recession Readiness Assessment of, 218-221

    as successful planner, 18, 20-21, 74-75, 94, 148, 161-163, 194

benchmarking, 28, 53-54, 64, 68, 86-87

Berkeley, Jay, 234

best practices, 19, 57, 110, 138, 141-142, 143, 198

betting the farm, 116, 120-121

BFC (Better, Faster, Cheaper), 143-144

Black Swan events, 45

The Black Swan (Taleb), 45, 214

Blazina, Kelly, 238

Blue Ocean concept, 66-67, 161-162, 164-165, 177-178, *182*

Blue Ocean Strategy (Kim and Mauborgne), 66, 161, 180-184, 214

BMW, 202

boards of advisors, 103-106

Bold Capital, 231

bonding companies, 100, 107

book clubs, 127-128, 161

borrowing from family, 13-15, 23, 165, 233

The Boys in the Boat (Brown), 127

brainstorming, 66, 129

bridge plans, 95-96

Brown, Daniel James, *The Boys in the Boat,* 127

Buczynski, Rick, "Flying Blind into the Next Recession?" 241

Buffett, Warren, 68, 114

BuiltWorlds, 231, 238

"Burnin' Down the House" (Powell), 239

Burnison, Gary, 161-162

  "Korn/Ferry's CEO on Transforming the Company in Mid-Crisis," 241

business hygiene. *see* best practices

C

C-players, 41, 128, 130-137, 204

Caesar's, 200-201

Camay, 202

canaries in the coal mine, 195-196. *see also* indicators, economic

cash, 101-103, 109, 153

cash flow, 86, 90, 94-95

casinos, 200-201

CEOs, 71, 190, 201

CFOs, 42, 98, 150, 155

Chait, Mark, 236

Chance, 239

Chang Sheppard, Jade, 236

Charan, Ram, *What the CEO Wants You to Know,* 128, 215

Choose Your Own Adventure, 26

CIT Group, 165

clients. *see also* customers

  accounting firms and, 107-108

  business relationships of, 53, 79, 124, 161, 183

  cash flow and, 109

  loss of, 78-79

  marketing for, 199-200

D

E

history of, 13-14, 90

Recession Readiness Assessment of, 222-225

values of, 66

flexibility, 75-76, 138, 146

"Flying Blind into the Next Recession?" (Buczynski), 241

Forbes, 144

Four Actions Framework, 180-184

The 4 Disciplines of Execution (McChesney, Covey, and Huling), 152, 216

4th Gear. *see* Accelerate

Frank L. Blum Construction, 78, 196

G

gaps, 54, 70-71, 115, 137-138, 164

GDP, 44

GE Capital, 114

Gentek Building, 237

geographical diversification, 169-170

Gluskin Sheff, 22

GM, 202

goals, 142, 145

The Goal (Goldratt), 143, 216

Golden Goose, 192-195

Goldratt, Eliyahu, *The Goal,* 143, 216

goods, durable and non-durable, 174

Gray, Matt, 238

Great Depression, 202

Great Recession (2008)

emotions during, 187-188

marketing and, 202

as misfortune, 13-14, 15, 58, 139, 170-171, 174, 194

as opportunity, 19-20, 57-58, 165, 171, 174, 230

green rating

in Accelerate, 167-168, 169

in Assess, 52-53, 62, 63, 70

Emergency Brake and, 191

in Race, 121-122, 142, 148, 151, 153

in Recession Readiness Assessment, 30

in Tune, 81-82, 86, 89, 92, 97-98, 100, 102, 103-104

Greenland, Don, 57-58, 84, 140, 193-194

grief stages, 187-189

Grisko, Jerry, 235

Grossman, Aaron, 236

growth, 86, 87-89, 93, 100-103, 122, 171, 176, 180

guest worker programs, 45-46

Gulati, Ranjay, "Roaring Out of Recession," 239

H

I

J

K

L

T

Z

CPSIA information can be obtained
at www.ICGtesting.com
Printed in the USA
LVHW031147300719
625788LV00001B/2